A Chal
Higher
Education
in Ontario

Edited by
Charles M. Beach

JOHN DEUTSCH INSTITUTE FOR THE STUDY OF
ECONOMIC POLICY, QUEEN'S UNIVERSITY

Published in cooperation with
McGill-Queen's University Press
Montreal & Kingston • London • Ithaca

ISBN: 1-55339-073-3 (bound)   ISBN: 1-55339-074-1 (pbk.)
© John Deutsch Institute for the Study of Economic Policy
Queen's University, Kingston, Ontario K7L 3N6
Telephone: (613) 533-2294   FAX: (613) 533-6025
Printed and bound in Canada

Library and Archives Canada Cataloguing in Publication

A challenge for higher education in Ontario / Charles M. Beach, editor.

Includes bibliographical references.

ISBN 1-55339-073-3 (bound)
ISBN 1-55339-074-1 (pbk.)

1. Rae, Bob, 1948- Ontario: a leader in learning. 2. Education, Higher--Ontario--Evaluation. 3. Provincial aid to higher education--Ontario. I. Beach, Charles M. II. John Deutsch Institute for the Study of Economic Policy.

LA418.O6C43 2005   379.1'224'09713   C2005-906370-X

Table of Contents

Acknowledgements   . . .   v

Introduction   . . .   1

**The Rae Review and the Structure of
Postsecondary Education in Ontario**   . . .   7
Michael L. Skolnik

**Assessing the Revenue Framework and
Multi-year Planning in the Rae Report**   . . .   27
Ken Snowdon

**The Rae Report and the Public Finance of
Postsecondary Education**   . . .   73
Robin Boadway

Accessibility in the Rae Report   . . .   97
Lorne Carmichael

Contributors

Acknowledgements

Preparation of this volume has benefited from the timely and thoughtful efforts of the contributing authors, and I wish to thank them very much for their contributions. I also wish to thank Sharon Sullivan of the John Deutsch Institute for her invaluable assistance throughout the project of producing this volume. Marilyn Banting provided excellent editorial services for the volume and Mark Howes of the Queen's Policy Studies Publishing Unit designed the cover. To all I wish to express my sincere appreciation for helping to bring this project to fruition.

Charles M. Beach
Director
John Deutsch Institute for the Study of Economic Policy
Queen's University

Introduction

In February 2005, Bob Rae presented *Ontario: A Leader in Learning —*
Report and Recommendations to the premier and the minister of training,
colleges and universities of Ontario following from the Rae Review of
higher education in Ontario. Within short months, in May 2005, the
Government of Ontario brought down a budget containing substantial
increases in postsecondary funding in the province and indicated their
intention to adopt many of the major recommendations of the report. Since
the demographic and funding environments in Ontario are shared by many
other provinces, it can be expected that the Rae Report will have a major
influence on the future of higher education, not just in Ontario, but in
Canada as a whole. The report addresses concerns of accessibility to
postsecondary education in the province, quality of the higher education
and training that is provided, current underfunding of universities and
colleges, availability of funds for eligible students, and accountability in the
postsecondary sector.

In light of the importance of the Rae Report, the John Deutsch Institute
at Queen's University approached several leading experts in the areas of
postsecondary education and its funding environment in Canada to write in-
formative reviews of the report. This volume presents their commentaries.
The objectives of the reviews are, first of all, to provide a critical
evaluation of the report's stance and recommendations for reform of the
postsecondary sector in Ontario. But the authors also seek to provide a
broader context in which to undertake such an evaluation and to suggest
alternative perspectives and recommendations to address the report's
concerns. Earlier this year, the John Deutsch Institute published a major
volume of studies on issues of postsecondary education in Canada —

Higher Education in Canada (2005), edited by C.M. Beach, R.W. Boadway, and R.M. McInnis — that effectively set the scene for the Rae Report. The present volume of reviews complements the above collection and should be viewed in the context of the major issues examined there of underfunding, student access, and faculty shortage.

This volume presents four reviews of the Rae Report from quite different perspectives. The first, by Michael Skolnik, focuses on what the report has to say about the general *structure* of postsecondary education in Ontario. Skolnik points out that the mandate of the Rae Review was to provide recommendations on the design of the public postsecondary education (PSE) system and on funding models for PSE, but the report concentrates much more on the latter and says rather little about the former. The report's funding recommendations for universities, for example, are based on comparisons with peer (public) institutions in the United States that are the most expensive institutions in the American PSE system which also includes a wide range of other PSE providers. While the report indeed advocates greater institutional differentiation, it does not convey a vision of what a differentiated system should look like or what kind of structural reforms are appropriate. Yet alternative funding mechanisms, controlled deregulation of tuition fees, proposed doubling of the number of graduate students, and mode of delivery of distance education in the province have potentially strong effects on the long-run structure of the PSE sector in Ontario. The new Council on Higher Education proposed in the report offers the potential to provide advice to the government on design of the higher education system. But the announced intention of the government in its May 2005 budget was to have the council focus on issues of accountability and quality improvement in PSE rather than on design or policy in the higher education system. The government may be losing an opportunity to undertake a major rethinking of what PSE structure would most benefit Ontario looking towards its future needs.

The second paper in the volume, by Ken Snowdon, assesses the revenue framework and funding proposals of the Rae Report. Snowdon notes that, over the past 40 years or so, the higher education system in Ontario has become "mass education" as participation rates in universities and colleges have increased dramatically. The government is thus faced with the challenge of how to fund a mass education system while ensuring accessibility, affordability (to both government and students), and an acceptable level of quality. The Rae Report proposes a new revenue framework for PSE institutions that offers them greater long-run funding security and predictability. Snowdon provides a useful review of past university funding arrangements in Ontario since 1967 as context for the Rae Review proposals. He notes that, while the title of the Rae Report is *A Leader in Learning*, the proposed funding levels are not in reference to benchmark leaders but to benchmark averages that Ontario should try to catch up with. He views the report's endorsement of the "corridor system" of funding as a positive move towards improved funding predictability.

Snowdon goes on to assess the funding mechanism the Rae Report proposes against the stated goals of access for all qualified students, quality of teaching and research, institutional autonomy within a public system, and the mutual responsibility of the players involved (government, institutions, and students). With respect to access, Snowdon notes that the Rae Report steps beyond the traditional Robarts policy of ensuring that Ontarians are provided the opportunity to pursue PSE. Higher education is now critical for prosperity of the province, and government must be proactive in encouraging participation in PSE. He also remarks that the report recognizes that access has several dimensions, including afford-ability, outreach, and capacity of the system. With respect to quality of teaching and research, the report recognizes that, in an environment of increased resources, across-the-board salary increases can leave little funding available for improvements in student-faculty ratios, enhancements of the teaching and research facilities, and basic infrastructure — hence the linkage of funding increases and accountability and multi-year revenue requirement plans by institutions. In return for greater public investment in the PSE system, institutions will have to demonstrate efforts to achieve government objectives of access, affordability, and improved quality of education.

The third paper in the volume, by Robin Boadway, examines the proposals of the Rae Report from the point of view of public finance principles. Boadway criticizes the report for its general lack of discussion of the underlying rationales for its various recommendations and for its relative lack of detail on how alternative policies might be designed to achieve the stated objectives of the report. It takes the existing PSE system as given and asks how it can be improved. Sweeping changes to institutions or methods of finance are not proposed; the approach to changes in funding is basically incremental. Perhaps this is to be expected given the time frame and resources of the review.

Boadway examines the rationales for government intervention in the provision of postsecondary education and their implications for government policy. With respect to policies applied to students, he identifies several difficult questions which need to be addressed such as what should be the share of PSE costs borne by students, how should the financing and risk costs to students be structured based on equity and efficiency criteria (say through an income-contingent loan program or graduate tax program), and more generally, how should PSE investments be treated by the income tax system? With respect to policies applied to PSE institutions, he raises further questions: How much decentralization of decision-making should exist in the PSE sector and to what extent should PSE institutions be free to decide tuition levels and programs to offer? How many students ought to receive higher education, what should the level of government funding be, and what factors should a funding formula take into account? Finally, Boadway calls for some rationalization of the federal and provincial roles and a clearer division of responsibilities in the Canadian PSE sector.

The fourth paper, by Lorne Carmichael, looks at the issue of accessibility as addressed in the Rae Report. Both Rae and Carmichael distinguish between access and affordability. High tuition fees certainly create a barrier for low-income students. However, the remedy is not to increase the tuition subsidy for everyone, but to focus attention on those in greatest need. Carmichael cites the report as clearly acknowledging that higher education overwhelmingly benefits upper-income families whose offspring enjoy a much higher participation rate in university education. He identifies two aspects of accessibility — capacity and equal access. Capacity of the system to offer positions to prospective students is addressed by a number of recommendations to increase funding levels to PSE institutions, thus make them more predictable, provide greater support for infrastructure, and subsidize increased graduate training. Equal access seeks to ensure that all qualified students can attend PSE institutions regardless of their ability to pay. This is addressed by savings plans and loans for those who can afford to pay and by targeted bursaries and grants for needy students. The report offers a number of strategies for reaching out to potential students from poor backgrounds. The report recommends an immediate expansion and revision of a PSE loan program and a longer-term development of a loan program with repayments based on income and made through payroll deduction as already adopted in several countries. This brings in the need for federal-provincial cooperation in implementing such a plan. Carmichael indeed recommends a move towards adopting a graduate tax where PSE tuition is free to all qualified students and graduates then pay a tax based on the tuition cost of their program and their actual income after graduating. Carmichael is very supportive of the Rae Report and feels that Rae has done a great service to postsecondary education in Ontario.

Charles M. Beach
Director
John Deutsch Institute for the Study of Economic Policy
Queen's University

The Rae Review and the Structure of Postsecondary Education in Ontario

Michael L. Skolnik

One of the major strategic choices facing a one-time advice-giver is how detailed and specific to make his or her advice. At one extreme he can concentrate on formulating general goals and principles, leaving the details to those responsible for implementing the recommendations. Alternatively, the advisor can set out a quite detailed blueprint that leaves little room for discretion by the policy actors. An advantage of the more detailed approach is that it limits the scope for those who receive the advice to interpret it in ways that were unintended by the advisor. A disadvantage is that it is impossible for the adviser to anticipate and account for the reactions of all the stakeholders and possible changes in the environment between the time that the advice is given and when action is finally taken. There is thus a risk that the general principles underlying the recommendations may be rejected due to unacceptability of the specific numerical parameters contained in the recommendations.

The final report of the Rae Review (Rae, 2005), hereinafter referred to as the report, contains a mix of very specific and very general recommendations, with the general recommendations in several cases being somewhat ambiguous. As an example of the first type of recommendation, not only does the report advocate providing grants to students from low-income families, but it specifies the precise level of family income below which students should be eligible for grants and the range for which they would be eligible for a mix of grants and loans. The report is also quite specific on the amount of additional funding that should be injected into post-secondary education in Ontario. In contrast, the recommendation concerning how this funding would be distributed among institutions is rather sketchy. Most of the recommendations are in the form of general statements of goals with the means for achieving the goals left somewhat vague. This will give lots of discretion to the government and to some of the stakeholders in developing the mechanisms and processes for implementation of the recommendations. It will also create a situation in which some of Bob Rae's intentions might be subverted.

Rae's mandate was to provide recommendations on two things: the design of the public postsecondary education system and funding models for postsecondary education.[1] Of the two, the report concentrates disproportionately on funding and rather neglects questions of design. Moreover, the report gives a lot of attention to something that was not an explicit element in its terms of reference, the proper level of funding for postsecondary education, as distinct from the funding framework. The report's concentration on funding levels and near silence on design has certainly pleased the universities. As one of Canada's leading higher education scholars, Professor Emeritus John Dennison of the University of British Columbia, is fond of pointing out, universities want only two things from government. One is money, the other is to be left alone. The Rae Report is essentially a strident public plea for more money for post-secondary education and a set of recommendations of varying detail on how to provide that money. In largely ignoring matters of design, the counsel of the report, implicitly at least, seems to be to leave the universities alone. Except for having only partial control over the setting of tuition fees, Ontario universities at present have almost complete autonomy. Rae's recommendation to deregulate tuition fees would remove the last limit on university autonomy in Ontario. Thus, the report would seem to satisfy Professor Dennison's notion of giving universities what they want: it gives them both more money and more autonomy!

---

[1]Specifically, the mandate was to provide recommendations on "the design of a publicly funded postsecondary system offering services in both official languages" and on "funding model(s) that link provincial funding to government objectives for postsecondary education". The mandate statement went on to include two areas of "secondary recommendations": the role of international students, and the role of marketing Ontario higher education internationally (Rae, 2005, p. 1).

Michael L. Skolnik

There are, however, two areas of recommendations that could impinge somewhat upon university autonomy. One of these pertains to accountability, the other to relations with the colleges. I will deal with the second area at greater length in the course of discussing what the report says about the role of colleges and college-university relations. First, I want to address the issue of accountability briefly.

It is no easy matter to sell the government or the public on a proposal to increase the funding of universities and colleges by as much as 50%. Beyond appealing to the concern for Ontario to be economically competitive with jurisdictions that are spending more than it does on postsecondary education, as the report does, I can think of only two strategies for making the funding recommendations palatable. One would be to ask universities and colleges to provide data that shows that the public will be getting good value for the additional funding that it is being asked to provide. This is the approach adopted in the report, as it observes that "the public and students will only be prepared to provide more funding if they see the value of the expenditure" (p. 16). An important theme of the report is to attempt to link increases in funding to measured improvements in quality.

The Rae Report acknowledges that increased demands for reporting could result in a diminution of institutional autonomy, but it cautions that this not be allowed to happen. So long as the government confines its demands for accountability to the collection of data on a limited number of performance indicators, institutional autonomy would not be threatened.[2] However, new requirements for program quality assessment could reduce institutional autonomy. This could possibly include the reference to "evaluating" quality, and the new "quality assurance framework" that are in the list of functions of the proposed new Council on Higher Education (p. 51).

A more likely problem with the report's recommendations regarding accountability is that they presuppose more than can be delivered. Although the report observes that the "assessment of the value of public expenditures when it comes to universities and colleges will not be easy" (p. 16), it fails

---

[2]For example, there is no evidence that the requirements for performance indicator data that the Harris government imposed on universities and colleges in the 1990s resulted in a significant reduction in institutional autonomy. In fact, simultaneously with imposing these new requirements for data, the government enacted new legislation for the colleges, one of the intentions of which was to give them greater institutional autonomy.

to show much appreciation of just how difficult this is. Higher education researchers have sought for a long time to measure quality and demonstrate the relationship between quality and funding, but this has turned out to be nearly impossible to do. Indeed, had it been possible to demonstrate the harmful effects of lower funding, which is the opposite side of the coin from the beneficial effects of higher funding, Ontario's universities and colleges might have been more successful over the past two decades in making their case for better funding.[3] And Bob Rae would have been able to use data on the harmful effects of the alleged underfunding to make his case for more funding, rather than having to rely on simple comparisons in funding levels with other jurisdictions.

The second approach to making the funding recommendations more palatable would be to persuade readers that Ontario's postsecondary education system presently is as efficient as possible, or failing that, to include some recommendations to increase efficiency, along with the recommendations for increased funding. This would involve dealing with the first of the two parts of Rae's mandate, the design of postsecondary education in Ontario, and addressing the question of whether there are structural changes that could make the design of Ontario's postsecondary education system more efficient.

As I have noted, Rae's funding recommendations were based largely on comparisons of funding levels between public universities in Ontario and peer institutions in selected American states.[4] However, he did not make any comparisons between Ontario and those states in regard to their respective structures of postsecondary education. Had he done so, one of the things that would have stood out is the wide range of providers of degree-level education in the United States compared to the situation in

---

[3]It was not for lack of effort that attempts to measure this relationship have been unsuccessful, but rather, because of the inherent conceptual and methodological problems (Skolnik, 1986).

[4]The report also considers the difference in funding levels between Ontario and other provinces. It notes that if Ontario universities were to be funded at the average per student level for other provinces in 2002/03, they would have needed an additional $300 million. The corresponding figure for community colleges was estimated to have been $400 million (Rae, 2005, p. 93). Given that the operating budget for the colleges was much less than for the universities, the relative amount by which the colleges were underfunded, in comparison with other provinces, was substantially greater than for the universities.

Michael L. Skolnik

Ontario. In most states, besides publicly funded comprehensive research-oriented universities, degree-level education is provided also by private degree granting institutions, publicly funded degree granting institutions whose mission is predominantly that of teaching, open and virtual universities, and community colleges. The existence of private degree granting institutions reduces the need that must be met by the public sector, thus enabling the state to provide higher per student funding for a given outlay of public funds than would otherwise be the case. The other forms of public provision of degree-level education offer the prospect of lower costs per student than the research university, which is the most costly of all models for the provision of undergraduate education, and the model upon which Ontario relies almost exclusively.

Deriving recommendations for provincial funding of universities on the basis of a simple comparison of funding levels between Ontario universities and peer institutions in the United States is of limited value insofar as the comparison fails to take account of differences in the context of the institutions being compared. The institutions with which the Ontario universities are compared are the most expensive institutions in the American system of postsecondary education that includes a diverse range of other less costly providers of undergraduate education; whereas in Ontario, these institutions are the only such providers. In basing his recommendations on this comparison, Rae is in effect arguing that all of Ontario's universities should be funded at the level at which the cream of the American system is funded. For supporters of higher education in Ontario, this would be a wonderful thing to see, but it is not apparent that any country in the world, the United States included, can afford such largesse.

It is important to take the structure of higher education into account, not only when considering funding levels but also funding mechanisms. The recommendation to give the universities control over the setting of tuition fees is one of the most important and most controversial proposals in the report. Not surprisingly, while the Ontario government has addressed many of Rae's recommendations in its May 2005 budget, it has thus far been silent on this and other questions pertaining to tuition fees. There is much to be said in favour of deregulation of tuition fees in terms of increasing economic efficiency and making the system more responsive to students. Unregulated fees are certainly appropriate in a postsecondary system like that of the United States which tolerates, if not celebrates, a high degree of institutional stratification. In Ontario, on the other hand, public policy has aimed to limit institutional stratification and foster a system that provides roughly comparable, though certainly not equal, opportunities for students regardless of which provincial institution they attend. Deregulation of tuition fees could undermine this public policy objective if it leads to a large spread in fee levels among institutions, and correspondingly in the resources that different institutions can provide and in the value of their degrees. On the other hand, that policy objective was established at a time when the overall size and cost of the university sector was much smaller than it is now, and it may no longer be a feasible objective.

Rae on Issues of Structure

Over the years, many observers have suggested modifying the design, or what I shall refer to as the structure, of higher education in Ontario in such a way as to make it more cost efficient. Suggestions for structural reform have included assigning a transfer role to the community colleges, changing the mandate of some universities to make them predominantly under-graduate teaching institutions, and establishing an open university. Pedagogically speaking, there are pros and cons to all these suggestions. What appealed to many of their proponents was that they were seen as a means to ensuring that Ontario could afford to fund at least a handful of its universities at a level comparable to the best in the world. Unless one assumes that unlimited public money is available for postsecondary education, all the alternatives to what the universities and Bob Rae deem to be an unacceptable status quo have serious downsides. The public reactions to the report demonstrate that even a proposal that includes an unprecedented increase in the operating grant has aspects that are quite objectionable to some stakeholders, particularly deregulation of fees combined with more emphasis on means-tested student financial assistance. Given that there is no totally happy choice to be made in this arena, it might have been useful to widen the range of options to include reforms of structure as well as reforms of funding, especially since both were part of the mandate of the Review.

Although the neglect of issues of structure in the report is regrettable, it is perhaps understandable. Rae was appointed to undertake this review in June 2004, and given that it would take some time to gear up at the beginning, and additional time to finalize and publish the report at the end, there was not a lot of time for such a large and complex project. Funding arrangements had to be given the priority, and just to complete such a detailed and thoughtful analysis of the funding options in the time available was a commendable accomplishment. I must add here that I was commissioned by the Rae Review to prepare a background paper on issues pertaining to the structure of postsecondary education in Ontario. Over my career, I have done enough research for provincial commissions and task forces to be neither surprised nor piqued when little of my work, or of the topic that I researched, made its way into the final report. Nor do I consider it appropriate or useful for me to use this essay as a vehicle for disseminating the content of the background paper that I did for the Rae Review, though some of the points made and issues raised in that paper will be included here when they are germane to this review of the report.[5]

The term, structure, is generally used in the literature of higher education to refer to the distribution of postsecondary institutions by type, mandate, and role within the system, and their relationships with one another. The analytical concept that is most central to the study of the structure of higher education is that of institutional differentiation. Thus, it was to the section entitled "Differentiation and Collaboration" that I looked first to see what the report had to say about structure. There I found that although greater institutional differentiation was advocated, no explanation was provided of what was meant by differentiation, nor was there a vision of what a differentiated system should look like. The report stated that "students benefit from differentiation" (p. 41), but what those benefits might be was not discussed. Also, the discussion failed to distinguish between differentiation *between* sectors (universities and community colleges) and differentiation *within* sectors. Often it was unclear which of these levels of differentiation was being referred to, though the report seemed to concentrate mostly on differentiation between sectors. The report made the important point — and made it eloquently — that differentiation and collaboration are, or should be, closely related, because the greater the institutional differentiation, the greater the need for collaboration between institutions. However, most of the section dealt with collaboration rather than differentiation.

Rather than offering any specific suggestions for differentiation, the report suggests means that might be employed to achieve greater differentiation. These included the tuition framework, accountability arrangements, and the funding formula. A problem, however, is that these

---

[5]This background paper has recently been published in an electronic journal (Skolnik, 2005).

mechanisms themselves were not described in sufficient detail for the reader to discern just how they could be used to promote greater institutional differentiation, let alone the specific types of differentiation that should be sought. Possibly the idea is that the funding formula could be redesigned in such a way as to provide incentives towards certain types of institutional differentiation, and that this could be reinforced through the multi-year planning and reporting processes. Going back to the distinctions made in the introductory paragraph of this essay, this would be an example of the report offering a general suggestion and leaving it to those who are responsible for implementation to determine how to implement the suggestion. However, because the report has provided no advice about what kind of structural reform would be desirable, there is insufficient guidance for the implementers to configure the incentives in the funding formula in such a way as to carry out the intentions of the advice giver. In summary, it is not clear just what, if anything, the report proposes in regard to institutional differentiation *within* either of the two postsecondary sectors, or how such differentiation might be achieved.

Specialization and Special Mission Institutions

One of the most basic decisions in the design of a system of postsecondary education is whether to have any special mission institutions, for example, those that concentrate on certain functions like undergraduate teaching; on a limited range of disciplinary fields like a technical university; or on serving a particular clientele, like the hearing impaired or people of particular language, culture, or religion. Creating special purpose institutions, or converting comprehensive institutions into special purpose institutions, is one of the most common ways of achieving greater institutional differentiation in postsecondary education. There are good arguments both in favour of, and against, special purpose institutions, and across North America over the past several decades, it is difficult to discern a trend towards or away from this form of institutional differentiation.[6]

---

[6]In one of the rare formal statements by an official body on this issue, the former Ontario Council on University Affairs recommended in favour of special mission institutions in the publicly supported degree-granting sector, but against independent single-discipline institutions (OCUA, 1991, pp. 16–17).

New ones have been created, like tribal colleges in the United States, while some formerly special purpose institutions have evolved towards having a more general, comprehensive mandate, like Ryerson University in Toronto. More than almost all other North American jurisdictions, Ontario has opted, in both the degree and non-degree sectors, for comprehensive postsecondary institutions that cover a wide range of functions, fields, purposes, and clientele. About the only exceptions to this general principle are the Ontario College of Art and Design, francophone colleges of applied arts and technology, and the University of Ontario Institute of Technology.

Given that there were several areas within the purview of the Rae Review where there has been some public discussion about the appropriateness of special mission institutions, or other types of variation in the present institutional arrangements, I was interested to see if the report offered any advice on the issue. In fact, the report gave considerable attention to the problems of both aboriginal and francophone students, but did not address the question of whether the existing institutional structures for serving those populations were the most appropriate. Concerns have been expressed that the existing approach to serving aboriginal students fails to validate indigenous knowledge and contains at least remnants of colonialism. That one of the briefs submitted to the Rae Review provided an impassioned argument as to why the American tribal college model was not appropriate to Canada suggests this is a model that at least some educators feel would help to improve educational outcomes for aboriginal students in Canada (Aboriginal Education Councils, 2004). Moreover, the existence of aboriginal controlled postsecondary institutions in Saskatchewan (First Nations University of Canada) and British Columbia (Institute of Indigenous Government) indicates that some provinces have opted for this model.

To take another example of a special mission institution, while emphasizing the need to improve teaching excellence and the quality of the undergraduate experience, the report does not mention the contribution that could be made towards this goal by the existence of degree-granting institutions that have a primarily undergraduate teaching mission. Indeed, the report takes the opposite approach in recommending a substantial increase in graduate enrolment which all universities would in principle be eligible to partake in. Noting that the participation rate in graduate education in Ontario is about half the rate in peer American states, the report advocates a doubling of the number of graduate students in Ontario universities over ten years. The recommendation that the funding for this expansion be provided to institutions on a proposal basis rather than by a distribution formula perhaps reflects some sympathy with the often heard criticism that resources for graduate studies in Ontario are too widely — and hence sparsely — distributed among the universities. However, the report does not come right out, as some educators have urged, and recommend greater concentration of graduate studies in a limited number of universities, or the creation of a world class centre for advanced studies in one university. Here again the report shows selective use of comparison with the United States. It concentrates on just the aggregate figures, ignoring the structural difference that resources for graduate education are far more concentrated in the United States than they are in Ontario.

Perhaps the biggest weakness of the report in the area of special mission institutions involves what it had to say about distance education. The report states that: "Distance education is key to the success of many students in Ontario who do not have access to a traditional campus" (p. 17), but it does not note that geographical distance from campus may be only one of several barriers to access, and not necessarily the most significant one. Many students are denied access because of inflexible admissions policies, inconvenient scheduling of courses, lack of credit transferability, and unavailability of programs that match the student's interest. A better descriptor than distance education for institutions that are dedicated to helping students overcome these barriers is an "open university". The hallmark of such institutions is not the technology they use, but their educational philosophy. Their philosophy emphasizes identifying and building upon the cognitive and experiential strengths of students, and they design their programs in flexible ways that meet student needs and foster student success. There is no existing Ontario university that has this type of institutional mission. That is not a criticism of any Ontario university, because they are all fulfilling other important missions. But from a system point of view, it is likely that we would be better off if Ontario students had better access to an open university.

Rae stated that while he "received some suggestions for a bold, new Ontario-based institution that would be dedicated to distance and on-line education", he rejected such a proposal because "it would be expensive and duplicative of what is already starting" (p. 17). Only if one fails to look past the technology and ignores differences in institutional mission, philosophy, and the way that an institution actually serves the student is it possible to say that Ontario universities are duplicating the function of an open university. And even in regard to the actual provision of on-line courses, there is a considerable difference between an institution that specializes in this form of delivery; recruits and trains faculty with this form of education in mind; has a substantial support infrastructure for on-line delivery; and has experience, protocols, and models for on-line delivery, and an institution where the design and provision of on-line courses is pretty much at the discretion of the individual faculty member, with varying and often limited institutional support for it.

The expense of establishing a new open university in Ontario would be a genuine concern, but fortunately there is no need for that. Canada already possesses one of the world's great open universities, Athabasca University in Alberta which already has been serving many students in Ontario. The market for an open university in Canada is not of such scale as to warrant the creation of an additional institution beyond the three that already exist (Athabasca, the Télé-université in Quebec, and the Open University in British Columbia[7]). All that would be needed would be to formalize a partnership between Ontario and Athabasca University, and perhaps with the Télé-université for francophone students. Athabasca University submitted a brief to the Rae Review in which it proposed such a partnership. In its brief, Athabasca suggested that Ontario might provide expedited treatment of Athabasca programs under the Post-Secondary Education Choice and Excellence Act, which would not have any financial cost; and contribute to the difference between the in-province tuition charged to Alberta students and the out-of-province tuition that the Alberta Legislature requires it to charge (Athabasca University, 2004). This would be an economically efficient way of meeting a need that is not met currently by Ontario universities.

The Role of Colleges and College-University Relations

As is well known, the original mandate of Ontario's colleges of applied arts and technology (hereinafter referred to as colleges) was to concentrate on career education and meeting the needs of youths who did not go on to university. However, over the years, the career fields for which the colleges historically have provided education have undergone considerable change, so that much higher levels of knowledge are required in those fields and in many of them the baccalaureate has become important for entry or

---

[7]The Open University in British Columbia is to be merged with University College of the Cariboo, to create the new Thompson River University.

advancement. The colleges have evolved in parallel with these career fields and now offer many programs at such a high level of expertise that they attract university graduates into them. On average in recent years, about twice as many students with university experience enter the colleges as students with college experience enter universities, and at one college about one in six students is a university graduate. Also, along with several other provinces and American states, Ontario colleges have been given authorization to award baccalaureate degrees in selected fields of applied study. As a result of the academic advancement which has occurred in the colleges, many college leaders have argued that not only do many college students need to be able to transfer to a university to complete a baccalaureate, but that these students have demonstrated in their college studies that they are capable of succeeding in university.

Although study in the colleges has been recognized for full academic credit, or close to it, by numerous universities outside Ontario, Ontario universities have in general not looked favourably on the academic advancement of the colleges. Leaders of Ontario universities have opposed the idea of colleges awarding baccalaureate degrees in applied fields of study, although, paradoxically, many of the assessors who have reviewed the proposals for these programs and recommended in favour of them are well-established professors in Ontario universities. Moreover, after years of exhortation from government, the reports of two government appointed inquiry bodies, and the establishment of a provincial level agency to promote transfer from community colleges to universities, the progress made to date in enabling students who start in a community college to complete a degree in a university has been rather meager.

It was against this background that leaders of each postsecondary sector made the case to Bob Rae for their view of the proper role of the colleges and the corresponding relationship between colleges and universities. In a perceptive commentary on this matter, *Toronto Star* columnist, Ian Urquhart described the problem of sorting out the claims of the colleges and universities as opening a can of worms (Urquhart, 2004). Urquhart summarized a "personal letter" to Rae from the President of the Council of Ontario Universities, Dr. Ian Clark, that the columnist noted was "making the rounds in the postsecondary community and causing a stir". In the letter, Dr. Clark expressed concern about the colleges becoming more like universities and argued that instead, colleges should concentrate on their original mandate of serving students who were not university-bound (Clark, 2004). Responding to the Clark letter, Joan Homer, CEO of the Association of Colleges of Applied Arts and Technology of Ontario (ACAATO), took issue with Clark's "two-silo" model of postsecondary education (Homer, 2004). Homer argued that because of the increasing knowledge and skill requirements of the workplace, many individuals who had originally attended a college might ultimately need access to a degree program and that they deserved such access at any time in their career. The Clark and Homer letters were but the tip of an iceberg in a longstanding dispute between the two sectors regarding the colleges' role with respect to degree-credit activity.

In adjudicating the dispute over the role of the colleges, Rae seemed to give something to each side. The description of the mandate that he proposes sounds awfully much like what Clark had advocated. Its emphasis is on "occupational" (not even "career") education, remedial education, serving the high school students who presently do not go on to any form of postsecondary education, and apprenticeship. There is no discussion of the college-degree programs except for saying that the government should continue to "allow" them. Rae refers to the original mandate of the colleges and says that it is as relevant today as it was in 1965. Nor does he discuss the changes that have occurred in work and society since 1965 that are relevant to the mandate of the colleges.

Where the report comes down on the college side of the dispute is in regard to its advocacy of credit transfer. Rae advises that the "government's approach in this area must be aggressive to stimulate real progress", though "balanced by respect for institutional autonomy and for the different mandates of Ontario colleges and universities" (p. 42). He suggests that government should consider the use of financial incentives and disin-centives to achieve collaboration between sectors, but does not say how such incentives and disincentives might be used. My view on this is that targeted financial incentives to universities for accepting transfer students from the colleges would stigmatize transfer students and invite definitional game playing in the funding formula, whereas simply changing the present corridor funding approach to an enrolment sensitive funding formula would do a lot to make transfer students more attractive to universities. Another option would be to modify the funding formula so that it gave some universities a greater incentive to expand undergraduate enrolment — which would include transfer students from the colleges — while it gave other universities a greater incentive to increase graduate enrolment. Such an approach would contribute to greater institutional differentiation within the universities of a type that could contribute to excellence in different functions.

In one of the toughest statements in the report, Rae states that: "If institutions cannot make progress under an umbrella of incentives, government should be prepared to mandate greater co-operation in the best interests of Ontario students" (p. 42). That sounds very much like a polite way of saying that if the universities won't agree to better degree-completion arrangements with the colleges of their own volition, the government should force them to do it. Two previous provincial reports in this territory have advocated that the government threaten the universities over the transfer credit issue, but in both cases the "or else" was to find some way for students to receive degrees for work done in the colleges.[8] The rigidity of the universities over the transfer credit issue led to this threat being invoked, in the form of the colleges being given the authority to grant baccalaureate degrees in a limited number of applied fields of study. But now that the colleges have been given the authority to grant degrees, this kind of threat would no longer work. So, unlike the earlier threats, the one in the report involves *forcing* the universities to do something rather than *letting* the colleges do something. However, given the sanctity with which governments of all political parties have treated university autonomy in Ontario — except in regard to setting their own tuition fees — it is anyone's guess whether this threat would ever be acted upon. Given that one of the main proposals in this section of the report is that the universities implement the very modest steps towards improving transfer credits that they agreed to in the Port Hope Accord six years ago and still have not implemented, the time for invoking this threat may not be far off.[9]

---

[8]Both the Vision 2000 (Ontario Council of Regents, 1990) and Pitman Task Force (Pitman, 1993) recommended that if satisfactory transfer arrangements could not be worked out with the universities, then some type of provincial consortium or agency with degree granting authority should be established through which degrees for programs done in whole or in part in the colleges could be awarded.

[9]The Port Hope Accord, formally titled The Ontario College-University Degree Completion Accord (1999), sets out targets for transfer credit and a process for achieving them. The Port Hope Accord is available in the Publications menu of the Web site of the College-University Consortium Council (http://cucc.cou.on.ca). While they viewed the Port Hope Accord as a useful starting point, the colleges have regarded the amounts of transfer credit indicated in that accord as inadequate.

Michael L. Skolnik

There is somewhat of a contradiction between the mandate that Rae recommends for the colleges, on the one hand, and on the other the strident call for the universities to recognize coursework done in the colleges for transfer credit. If the colleges concentrate on remediation, apprenticeship courses, and low level occupational training, then the universities would be absolutely correct in questioning whether the coursework in the colleges is of a level to justify generous transfer credit. In this regard, Dr. Clark has helped to move the debate forward by emphasizing the need for consistency between the role assigned to the colleges and their relationship with the universities. But by emphasizing the Clark vision for colleges, rather than the Homer vision in his discussion of the role of colleges, the report undermines the case for improved transfer arrangements while at the same time it advocates it.

The remedial, high school liaison, and more basic level vocational training activities that the report emphasizes are important, but so too are the higher level career education activities of the colleges. As colleges increasingly operate programs on the frontier of technical education in a wide range of career fields, and at the same time become more involved in applied research related to those career fields, their span of activity may become a more troubling issue. It may be that some colleges should concentrate on polytechnic education while others concentrate more on the types of activities that comprise the bulk of the discussion of the college mandate in the report. Or perhaps, other public agencies should undertake many of the important activities advocated by Bob Rae, like the way that these activities are divided up in Alberta between Alberta vocational centres and community colleges. These are vital issues in the design of Ontario higher education that also have major implications for the relationship between colleges and universities. At present there is no forum or means for getting them onto the policy agenda, let alone addressing them.

The Council on Higher Education

The most important advice that the Rae Review offers regarding the design of the higher education system is contained under the rubric of its proposal for a new Council on Higher Education. In elaborating on the role of the council, the report argues that postsecondary education institutions are constantly changing, and that there is a need for a well-informed, objective body to be continuously monitoring these changes and providing advice to the government on the evolution of the postsecondary system. An example is given that relates to one of the structural issues that I discussed at the end of the previous section, a community college evolving into a polytechnic, degree-granting institution.

The section of the report that pertains to the council does a lot to complete the discussion of structure. One can reasonably infer from what the report says about the council that Rae made a quite deliberate decision not to try to answer the kinds of specific questions about structure that I posed earlier, but instead to propose a funding framework and policy analysis mechanism through which such questions could be addressed effectively in due time. Going back to the distinction that I made at the beginning of this essay between providing a blueprint and providing a framework for subsequent decision-making, this was certainly a responsible choice. However, handing off a legacy to a proposed successor does, as I noted earlier, carry certain risks. In this case, one is that the government may choose not to accept this recommendation at all. The other is that, if established, the council may not operate as Rae envisions, or it may be swamped with the other tasks that he envisages for it, or that others assign to it.

The other key responsibilities of the proposed council would include "monitoring, evaluating, and publicly reporting on quality and system performance, leading to a new quality assurance framework"; "advising on performance measures and improvement mechanisms suitable for inclusion in multi-year plans"; "collecting critical benchmark data on key aspects of higher education"; and "leading a renewed focus on the pre-eminence of teaching and teaching excellence at postsecondary institutions". With the heavy emphasis on quality related matters, there is a danger that the council could become a second quality assessment agency, when what is needed most is a broader higher education policy advisory body.[10] In fulfilling the latter function, the council would be a highly visible advice-giving body that, unlike previous postsecondary agencies, would have purview over all of postsecondary education; in fact, examining and advising on collabora-

---

[10]The Post-Secondary Education Quality Assessment Board (PEQAB) has responsibility for advising the minister on applications to offer degree programs in Ontario from out-of-province degree-granting institutions wishing to offer programs in Ontario; Ontario-based private institutions; and Ontario community colleges that seek to offer applied baccalaureate programs. It would not be prudent for another provincial agency to attempt to duplicate the expertise that the PEQAB has developed in regard to quality assessment.

Michael L. Skolnik

tion between sectors would be one of its highest priorities. It would be constituted on the basis of expertise rather than constituency representation; look at the big picture and take a long-term view; and both advance and draw heavily upon research.

In its May 2005 budget, the government announced its intention to establish the Higher Education Quality Council of Ontario. This announcement was included in the budget document that described how the government intended to deal with the recommendations of the Rae Review (Ontario Ministry of Finance, 2005). The new council was listed under the heading, Accountability, where it was said that it would "take a lead role in supporting quality improvement in postsecondary education". There was no mention of any role for the new council with regard to design or policy in Ontario higher education.

It is still perhaps too early to tell whether the role of the new council will be, as its name and the description in the budget suggest, confined to quality assurance. No doubt this is what the universities would prefer. While their brief to the Rae Review advised against the establishment of *any* new provincial agency at all (Council of Ontario Universities, 2004, pp. 23-24), they could certainly accept a body whose mandate is narrowly confined to accountability if that is a necessary condition of getting a substantial increase in funding, as appears to be the case. In contrast, the Association of Colleges of Applied Arts and Technology of Ontario (ACAATO) recommended the establishment of an "independent" higher education agency with a broad mandate that would include strategy, policy, and funding advice. ACAATO further recommended the establishment of another body under the umbrella of the higher education agency that would work to improve transfer credit (ACAATO, 2004, p. 5).

At a luncheon shortly after the budget, held by ACAATO to celebrate the fortieth anniversary of the legislation that established the CAATs, the minister acknowledged that of the two tasks that it was given, the Rae Report concentrated mainly on funding and largely ignored design.[11] She said that the government intended to address issues of design, but did not say whether design would be part of the mandate of the Higher Education Quality Council, or would be addressed by some other means. For example,

---

[11]The luncheon, entitled the "May 21, 1965 Recognition Luncheon", was held at George Brown College on May 18, 2005. It was on May 21, 1965 that the minister of education, the Hon. William Davis, introduced the legislation for the CAATs.

the policy and design issues that Bob Rae placed within the mandate of his proposed Council on Higher Education could instead be assigned to the ministry. Likely though, this alternative would be a prescription for the status quo. With the best of intentions, and even with the promise of a modest increase in funding for research, a ministry is inherently unable to stand "somewhat removed from the daily fray", as Rae has rightfully said is necessary for an advice-giver.

Rae's call for a council to deal with structural and policy issues hardly comes out of the blue. Almost 40 years ago, the Spinks Commission found it "striking" that there was not a provincial agency in Ontario that could articulate a vision or plan for postsecondary education in the province (Spinks, 1966). Since then, numerous task forces, committees, and commissions have advocated the establishment of a provincial body to provide direction and coordination for the postsecondary education system, but these calls have been conspicuously disregarded (Royce, 1997). The threat now is that yet another call for this type of agency will either be disregarded, or that the important need identified by Spinks and numerous other advisers will take a distant back seat to attempts at quality measurement. Although a quality measurement agency may have some political appeal, the experience of such initiatives elsewhere suggests that it is a poor use of limited resources, and could even have some harmful effects (Bruneau and Savage, 2002).

In just a few months, with a limited amount of research support, Bob Rae has demonstrated what can be accomplished by an objective inquirer who has good listening skills in addressing seemingly intractable problems of postsecondary education. In the best scenario, the proposed council would flesh out, extend, and refine the many valuable suggestions in the report, and help us advance on the journey that Rae has started. However, if the mandate of the new council is instead restricted to, or heavily concentrated upon, simply reporting on quality, there is a good chance that the job that he has begun will remain unfinished.

References

Aboriginal Education Councils in Partnership with Cambrian College, Canadore College, Confederation College, George Brown College, Georgian College, Sault College. 2004. *A Vision for Aboriginal Post-Secondary Education* (November 30). On-line submission to the Rae Review, at http://www.raereview.on.ca.

Association of Colleges of Applied Arts and Technology of Ontario (ACAATO). 2004. *Achieving High Expectations in Ontario's Postsecondary Education Sector: A Plan for Change* (November). Toronto: ACAATO.

Athabasca University. 2004. *Submission to the Rae Commission* (December). On-line submission to the Rae Review, at http://www.raereview.on.ca.

Bruneau, W. and D. Savage. 2002. *Counting Out the Scholars: How Performance Indicators Undermine Universities and Colleges.* Toronto: James Lorimer.

Clark, I. 2004. Letter to The Honourable Bob Rae (October 14).

Council of Ontario Universities. 2004. *A Vision for Excellence: COU Response to the Postsecondary Review Discussion Paper* (October 29). Toronto: COU.

Homer, J. 2004. Letter to Mr. Ian Clark (October 29).

Ontario Council of Regents. 1990. *Vision 2000: Quality and Opportunity. A Review of the Mandate of Ontario's Colleges.* Toronto: Ministry of Colleges and Universities.

Ontario Council on University Affairs (OCUA). 1991. *Advisory Memorandum 91-V. The Establishment and Development of Provincially-Assisted Degree-Granting Institutions in Ontario.* Toronto: OCUA.

Ontario Ministry of Finance. 2005. *Reaching Higher: The McGuinty Government Plan for Postsecondary Education. 2005 Ontario Budget Backgrounder.* At http:www.ontariobudget.fin.gov.on.ca.

Pitman, W. (Chair). 1993. *No Dead Ends: Report of the Task Force on Advanced Training to the Minister of Education and Training.* Toronto: Ministry of Education and Training.

Rae, The Honourable Bob (Adviser to the Premier and the Minister of Training, Colleges and Universities). 2005. *Ontario: A Leader in Learning. Report and Recommendations.*

Royce, D. 1997. *University System Coordination and Planning in Ontario, 1945–1996.* Toronto: University of Toronto. PhD dissertation.

Skolnik, M.L. 1986. "If the Cut is So Deep, Where is the Blood? Problems in Research on the Impact of Financial Restraint", *The Review of Higher Education* 9(4), 435–455.

_____. 2005. "A Discussion of Some Issues Pertaining to the Structure of Postsecondary Education in Ontario and Some Suggestions for Addressing Them", *College Quarterly* 8(1). At http://www.senaca.on.ca/quarterly.

Spinks, J.W.T. (Chair). 1966. *Report to the Committee on University Affairs and the Committee of Presidents of Provincially-Assisted Universities of the Commission to Study the Development of Graduate Programs in Ontario Universities.* Toronto: The Commission.

Urquhart, I. 2004. "Colleges, Universities Gird for Fight", *Toronto Star*, November 10, p. A29.

Assessing the Revenue Framework and Multi-year Planning in the Rae Report

Ken Snowdon

Introduction

Ontario: A Leader in Learning (Rae Report) is the latest of a long series of reports about various aspects of postsecondary education in Ontario. Every several years, it seems, government is destined to turn to a commission to help sort out the challenges of the day in the postsecondary sector. What are those challenges? They usually centre around meeting enrolment demand (accessibility), the level of tuition and aspects of student assistance (affordability), and the need to improve the learning environment (quality). They also seem to lead to calls for increased levels of funding and greater accountability. The government of the day may also have a few specific issues — college/university collaboration, whether to encourage private institutions or not, what to do to correct decreasing demand in certain parts of the province — that happen to be on the minister or premier's desk at the time the commission is established.

Each of the many reports has had an impact; some more than others. The impact — whether it be new policies, more funding, new funding mechanisms, new directions, shifts in direction, or new reporting requirements — has contributed to the ongoing, seemingly never-ending change in postsecondary education in Ontario. At one level that change can, and should, be seen as sweeping. Over the past 40 years or so, higher education in Ontario has become "mass education".[1] The college system is now a vital part of the postsecondary landscape and an integral part of many communities across the province. Universities have grown in number, size, and importance and in the process moved "from private domain to public utility" (Corry, 1970, p. 101, quoted in Jones, 2005, p. 174).

As a public utility government has taken considerable interest in regulating universities (and colleges) and using the funding mechanism(s) and funding levels as the instruments of government policy — with special emphasis on ensuring accessibility and controlling the price to students and their families (affordability). For most of the past 40 years or so the price of education has been regulated — both tuition and the government subsidy. In more recent times, government provided limited "deregulation" of tuition but within a relatively short period of time "re-regulated". With the exception of very few programs (e.g., Executive MBA) tuition is still subject to government regulation via a two-year freeze (2004/05 and 2005/06) implemented by the Liberal government. The other part of price is the level of government subsidy, which in *real terms* on a *per student* basis has been on a downward trend since the 1970s. Government's conundrum has been how to fund a mass education system that ensures accessibility, is affordable, (to both government and students), and offers an acceptable level of quality.

In the early 1960s, Premier John Robarts stated that it was the government's intention to ensure that there was room "within our universities for all students who wish to proceed to some form of higher education".[2] Governments of all political stripes have grappled with funding that commitment ever since and used a variety of approaches that have ultimately resulted in an increased proportion of the cost being borne by students and their families, continuing concerns about quality, and constant pressure for more government funding.[3] On the way the university sector has been wracked by shifts in provincial funding policy and a

---

[1] Trow (1974) suggests the transition from élite to mass education occurs at about 15% of the relevant age group. As reported in Johnstone (1998).

[2] Statement to the Legislature of Ontario, by Premier John Robarts, March 21, 1963 as quoted in Cameron and Royce (1996).

[3] Other provinces have tended to opt for an access policy that sets limits on the number of available university spaces.

planning environment that in more recent times could best be characterized as "chaotic".

The nature of the federal presence in the postsecondary sector changed markedly as well. Federal-provincial fiscal arrangements evolved from 50/50 cost-sharing to unconditional grants that had little to do with the needs of the postsecondary sector. Changes in federal transfer arrangements have created fiscal challenges for the province that have affected the level of operating support at the institutional level. In the past decade, calls for more federal funding to meet postsecondary demands spawned a set of direct investment programs, such as the Canada Foundation for Innovation (CFI), and the Canada Research Chairs (CRCs), aimed specifically at the institutions, but carrying conditions that required provincial contributions. At the same time, the federal government increased payments to individuals through various tax credits, changes in the Canada Student Loan Program, new scholarship programs and the establishment of the Canada Millennium Foundation. The increased federal presence is distinctly different than it was, it created its own set of challenges, and, in more recent years, added to the general sense of turmoil that has characterized the postsecondary sector.

One of the most interesting aspects of the Rae Report is that Bob Rae has seen the damage caused by government actions (or inaction). In the case of the provincial government his "fix" is to establish a legislative framework to enshrine key principles and lessen the vagaries and vicissitudes of government legislators and bureaucrats. That fix, coupled with a proposed new Revenue Framework — that, among other things recognizes the important role of the federal government — are core components of *Ontario: A Leader in Learning*. His response to the changes in the federal presence are sharp and clear: restore the real value of the Canada Social Transfer. Rae's report is impressive, structured around three overarching goals, seven key strategies, and twenty-eight recommendations involving $2.1 billion in *new* investment over the next three years, and the establishment of a legislative framework that "sets out the parameters of the student assistance program, the frameworks for revenue — including tuition — and accountability, and mandated public reporting of performance and results" (Rae, 2005, p. 29).

Whether some or all of the recommendations will be partially or wholly implemented is in the hands of the McGuinty government. The focus of this paper is twofold: to review the implications of the Rae Report's proposed Revenue Framework; and to assess the proposed accountability mechanisms. In both cases emphasis will be placed on the implications for universities. To explore both of these topics in some depth, it is important to have an understanding of university funding in Ontario and the existing accountability practices.

Background

University Funding

Taking Stock: Assessing the Current Financial Situation. According to the findings in the Rae Report the funding "gap" between Ontario universities and other provinces is estimated to be about $380 million for 2004/05. Relative to the United States, Rae estimates the gap ranges from about $900 million to $1.8 billion and settles on a figure of $1.4 billion.

Since the mid-1980s, university funding in Ontario has been characterized by major shifts in the sources of funding: provincial operating grants represented about 75% of operating funding in 1987 versus about 50% in more recent times. Fees represented about 20% of operating income in 1987 and now constitute about 45% of operating income.

Over the past decade, tuition increases have been de-coupled from the provincial funding formula. That change in the funding formula, coupled with increased operating grants for additional enrolments, means that there is currently a direct link between the income a student generates (tuition and grant) and income an institution receives; the existing funding mechanisms are enrolment sensitive.

Pressure points have arisen because the total level of funding has not kept pace with cost increases and enrolment growth. Accessibility increases have occurred at the expense of quality considerations, thus leading to increased class sizes, less student to faculty interaction and fewer opportunities for real student engagement.

Pressure points have also arisen because, since the early 1990s, government financing has been characterized by changing funding policies and unexpected changes in funding mechanisms. Together, those factors — cost pressures, enrolment growth, decreases in grant funding per student in real terms, and changes in funding mechanisms — have contributed to a very unpredictable and straitened financial environment. To understand the full import of Rae's recommendations it is necessary to have some understanding of the funding mechanisms that have characterized provincial funding allocations.

Formula Financing. Ontario was one of the first jurisdictions in Canada to adopt formula financing in the university sector and many of the basic concepts that underpinned that development are still operative today. From the outset it is critically important to distinguish the role of formula financing in the allocation or distribution of funding versus its role in determining the level of funding. Formula-funding models tend to be focused on the distribution or allocation of specified levels of government funding. While such a formula may have some links to actual costs and hence be seen, by some, as having a major impact on the overall level of resources that should be provided to a specific entity (schools, universities, colleges, hospitals, municipalities, etc.), the fact is that government sets the actual level of funding based on a host of factors including cost pressures, competing priorities, government objectives, the state of the economy, and the state of government finances. The formula is simply the allocation device, but the way it is designed can have steering effects on the recipients and thus it can become an instrument of government policy.

Formula-funding models tend to be designed with specific principles in mind as follows:

Equity: the formula strives to achieve equitable allocations based on common quantifiable factors (i.e., enrolment, classroom space per student);

Predictability: the formula is designed to allow for a high degree of predictability in overall funding;

Stability: the formula tends to be designed to provide smooth transitions to changes in funding distribution and allocation;

Accountability: through the use of simple inputs (i.e., enrolment, space per student, space per faculty) formula funding provides an easy to understand part of the accountability framework (of course that should be augmented by outcome reports, public financial reporting, and the easy availability of measures that can be used to determine if the funds are achieving intended objectives);

Simplicity / Transparency: the formula tends to be easy to explain and understand and the factors that trigger changes in allocations have clear rationale;

Effectiveness: the formula may be designed to achieve government objectives through the use of factors that influence specific parts of the allocation (i.e., enrolment); and

Efficiency: through the design of the formula, efforts are made to ensure that incentives are in place to promote efficiencies and/or disincentives are in place to prevent inefficient practices.

In effect, formula financing attempts to provide a level playing field and well-defined rules of the game so that the affected entity (schools, colleges, universities, hospitals, municipalities) can plan in an orderly fashion and seek to accomplish its objectives (and government objectives) in an effective and efficient manner.

Usually the formula approach is centred around a basic grant or core grant that is based on a common set of input factors and some notion of average costs. Those characteristics assume a certain degree of homogeneity of institutional mission. Special grants are then used to address specific issues that may affect the recipients differentially. Those special grants will often be allocated based on a formula mechanism as well.

The history of formula financing in Ontario has been chroniclled at different times in a number of places (Council of Ontario Universities, 2004a; Darling *et al.*, 1989; Leslie, 1980) thus what follows is a brief overview intended to provide sufficient context for the discussion of the Rae proposals. To help illustrate the major changes in the funding formula (the allocative mechanism) and the factors influencing those changes, Figure 1 attempts to provide a composite overview.[4] A careful review of the figure provides a glimpse of the major changes that have occurred over the past 40 years, spanning various governments. Enrolment increased markedly over the period as did participation rates, even in the face of decreases in the 18 to 24-year-old population. There are a few periods where enrolment actually decreased (1976–79) or remained relatively flat

---

[4]Figure 1 is an updated and augmented version of a graph in the Council of Ontario Universities (2001).

Figure 1: Funding, Enrolment and Participation Rates, Ontario 1967 to 2004

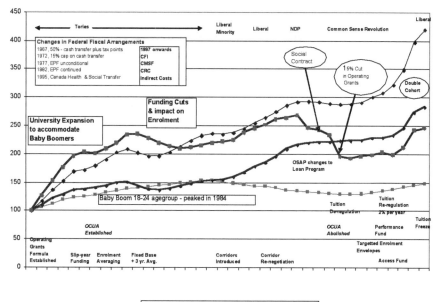

(1984–86 and 1993–98). Interestingly enough those downturns or steady-state periods matched downturns in provincial funding (often influenced by changes in federal transfer payments) or formula changes that dampened the relationship between enrolment change and provincial funding. As long as the relationship between enrolment increases and funding is reasonably strong the evidence suggests the universities will increase enrolment and meet the demand (Snowdon, 2004).

What is masked in Figure 1 are the machinations involved in trying to ensure student demand is legitimate and not just induced by the institutions in an attempt to garner more funds, and trying to get the universities to take more students (access) at the lowest cost to government. Accessibility and affordability have been the preoccupation of government, easy to define and politically important. It is not surprising then, that the basic funding formula in Ontario focused on student enrolment and incorporated tuition into the equation. The evolution of formula financing and the history of government funding in the university sector are worthy of a brief review because both elements play major roles in setting the context for the Rae Review.

In the beginning... Prior to 1967, individual universities went "cap in hand" to the minister of the day and made their specific request for government support.[5] Institutional grants were essentially a series of private bilateral negotiations between representatives of an institution and representatives of the Ministry of University Affairs. This approach had its shortcomings, as noted in a Council of Ontario Universities' paper on the subject:

> the amount of effort required by both institutions and government, the latter of course having to repeat the effort for each institution; the Ministry's review of a detailed institutional budget submission was regarded by institutions as an infringement of autonomy; open public accountability was not consistent with private negotiations; there was no obvious or easy way in which to demonstrate equity in budget allocations among institutions, even assuming such equity existed; and, since the players and political imperatives could change from year to year, there was little or no predictability of available resources on which to base long range or even short range planning. (Council of Ontario Universities, 2004a, pp. 1-2)

The expansion of the Ontario university system in the latter part of the 1960s necessarily led to a major reform in university financing; the adoption of an enrolment-based funding formula that considered both provincial grants and tuition in the equation. Based on concepts articulated by the Bladen Commission (Commission to the Association of Universities and Colleges of Canada, 1965), a funding formula was developed by assigning funding weights (basic income units) for each program based on estimates of program cost.[6] Each institution's enrolment was multiplied by

---

[5]Starting in 1967 federal-provincial arrangements changed so that provinces would receive federal funding to cover 50% of the provincial post-secondary expenditures.

[6]From their inception, the BIU weights were meant to be a rough "proxy" for differences in average program cost and were derived, principally, from looking at the relationship of funding to program enrolments at several of the established universities at the time. The average program cost approach, however, did not adequately meet the needs of smaller institutions nor those with differentiated missions and quickly led to a requirement for additional funding. Initially called "supplementary grants", those allocations became institutionalized as "mission-

the program weights and the resultant total was known as an institution's basic income units or BIUs.

The actual grant per university was then determined by multiplying the *number* of BIUs by the *value* of the BIU. The value of the BIU included both the provincial grant and a government determined tuition called the "standard fee". While an institution could charge a higher tuition, the government simply deducted the higher tuition from the provincial grant. Through this mechanism, government effectively controlled the two major sources of revenue. In effect, students in the same program were funded at exactly the same level across all the institutions in the province. A history student at Trent attracted the same amount of grant and tuition funding as a history student at Windsor, or Queen's or Waterloo. The adoption of this approach was a clear indication that the funding mechanism was not a tool for differentiation; differentiation would occur through system-wide planning and institutional role differentiation.

In general, the universities were satisfied with the formula. The overall level of funding was sufficient to meet budgetary requirements, the formula was simple, tied directly to student enrolment and, more or less, recognized differences in program costs.[7] Government, however, very quickly saw the need for modification. The original formula was open-ended — that is, every student generated a provincial grant (and tuition). The fact that the annual cost to the province was not known until all students had enrolled caused some concern with provincial officials.[8] Accordingly in the early 1970s the province began funding enrolment on a "slip-year" basis; that is with a one-year lag. Such an adjustment improved funding predictability for both government and universities. However, within a very short time the concept of slip-year was replaced with averaging enrolments over a three-year period (1976) and then government introduced the concept of a fixed enrolment base (a specified time period) and a moving average with discounts applied to enrolment changes (1978). In effect, government, with

---

related" grants. For details about supplementary grants and BIU weights, see MTCU, Universities Branch (2004).

[7]While there was general agreement with the "weights" that had been assigned to programs, there were a number of "weight" changes that occurred in the first few years after the introduction of the formula.

[8]At the same time, the federal government introduced a "cap" on the annual increase in the cash transfer.

the advice of the recently established Ontario Council on University Affairs (OCUA), was formally acknowledging the concept of fixed and marginal costs. With the impact of the "baby boom" coming to an end, universities were somewhat more amenable to accepting changes in the formula that would provide a buffer against enrolment declines. For a few years enrolment actually decreased and the funding arrangement seemed even more attractive. Government, having had another adjustment to the federal transfer arrangements was looking for ways to contain the increase in government spending. Little did either level of government or the universities expect that within a few short years participation rates would increase and more than compensate for the projected decrease in the 18 to 24-year-old population (see Figure 1).

Corridor Funding. Following the Commission on the Future Development of the Universities of Ontario (Bovey Commission) the link between current enrolments and provincial grants was lessened further by the adoption of enrolment funding "corridors" in the mid-1980s. Essentially, as long as a university was within + or − 3% of the corridor mid-point (defined by the number of BIUs), the operating grant would remain intact. If enrolment dropped below the specified level by 3% or more, the grant would be reduced. There was also provision to increase the funding for institutions that increased their enrolment by more than 3% but, in fact, those provisions were never implemented by government, thus contributing to later claims regarding "unfunded BIUs". The work of the Bovey Commission also led to the introduction of additional targeted envelopes such as the Research Overheads/Infrastructure Envelope (ROIE) that explicitly recognized federal granting agency funding in the allocation formula.

A major expansion of the university system in the late 1980s, fuelled by increased participation rates and secondary school reform, led to a renegotiation of the corridor mid-points for each university. Government provided additional funding for the increased enrolment and also set specific enrolment targets in a select set of program areas. At the same time government provided separate funding for faculty renewal and other special initiatives. As the universities headed into the 1990s there was general satisfaction with the funding *mechanism*, the corridor system was a demonstrated success and the targeted envelopes provided government with sufficient flexibility to announce special initiatives and be seen to address specific concerns. Government grants peaked in the early 1990s. From that point onwards the overall funding environment changed dramatically.[9]

Constraint, Contraction and the Common Sense Revolution. The New Democratic Party (NDP) time frame is best remembered for government expenditure restraint and the Social Contract. In light of a provincial economic slowdown, various measures were taken to reduce the rate of increase in government program expenditures. Student aid was reformed with loans replacing grants. Additional Qualifications Courses for teachers were deemed ineligible for government funding. Annual increases in operating grants were replaced with absolute decreases. Under the Social Contract, "Rae days" became a form of currency. Government intervention on funding matters and governance was the order of the day. By the time the NDP left office formula financing was still in place but it was clear the government could (and would) change the rules of the game, frequently, sometimes with consultation and sometimes without. It was equally clear that the province's fiscal position was tenuous and would be a major pre-occupation of the Common Sense Revolution led by Mike Harris.

By the mid-1990s the Harris Tories had replaced the Rae government and the first order of business was to rein in the mushrooming provincial deficit and deal with impending cuts in federal transfer payments. In the post-secondary sector that translated into a major (15%) cut in the level of provincial operating grants and provision to allow institutions the opportunity to recoup some of the loss by increasing tuition and keeping the additional tuition income.[10] The Tory philosophy was to provide the "tools" for the public sector to become more market-oriented (Ibbitson, 1997,

---

[9]For a glimpse into the magnitude of the change and its impact on government policy, see Rae (1997).

[10]In fact, there had been very small moves in that direction by the previous governments. While fees were an integral part of the total funding formula, as early as 1980/81 the Tory government had allowed institutions the leeway of charging and keeping 10% more than the stated "regulated" fee. After a review of ancillary fees in the mid-1980s the Liberal government increased this so-called "discretionary" portion of the fee by an additional three percentage points. That allowable increase was meant to compensate for restrictions on the amount of "ancillary fee" that an institution could charge. However, both initiatives provided precedents for a shift in government policy — that is, the sum of grant and tuition funding was no longer intended to be equal across programs and institutions.

p. 132) and begin the process of launching major reform. In the case of universities that meant several things: letting universities increase tuition (in a "regulated" fashion); shifting the student aid burden associated with tuition hikes to the universities, removing international students from the funding formula; and launching the Advisory Panel on Future Directions for Postsecondary Education (Smith Panel) in the summer of 1996.

Later that year the Smith Panel filed its report *Excellence, Accessibility, Responsibility*, and re-affirmed the merits of the enrolment-corridor funding system and also recommended that tuition for Canadian students should be further "deregulated". The minister of the day, John Snobelen, added fuel to the general state of disquiet by his infamous quote about the need to "invent a crisis" (ibid., p. 222). Even though it was not directed at the university sector, the minister's sentiments reinforced the view that further reform was going to be the order of the day. Moreover, with the demise of the Ontario Council on University Affairs — a casualty of budget cuts and institutional antipathy — the way was left open for government to become directly active in the policy field. Downsizing, restructuring, tuition increases, a government advisory panel, changes in funding policy and a minister with little time for universities, combined to create a tumultuous situation on campuses across the province. While universities had been silent on the abolition of the Ontario Council on University Affairs, the absence of a "buffer body" was noticeable and *Excellence, Accessibility, Responsibility* spoke to the need for a postsecondary advisory body (recommendation 13) — a recommendation the government ignored.

Given the pressure on institutional finances since the early 1990s, constant calls for greater efficiency and downsizing, and a general sense that government had little time for universities, the university sector felt somewhat beleaguered. Staff and faculty railed against cutbacks and salary restraint. Students railed against tuition hikes (and so did faculty and staff in some institutions). Job losses created undue tension on campuses across the province. Against that background it should not be surprising that the mid-90s also witnessed the emergence of more faculty unions and union drives on more campuses.[11]

By 1998, government had adopted parts of specific recommendations from the Smith Panel and announced further deregulation of tuition in certain programs, although the government used the term "additional cost-

---

[11]Queen's (1996), Western (1997), and a unionization vote at Waterloo in the same period.

recovery".[12] Deregulation was consistent with the Tory philosophy, although the backlash from students was more than anticipated. The university community, still reeling from the cuts in provincial grants and coping internally with the aftermath, was thrown into an environment that could be best characterized as chaotic. The deregulation of tuition created an enormous amount of controversy on some campuses. Yet, in the absence of any additional grant monies to meet normal cost increases, the universities had to rely on major tuition fee hikes to help meet budgetary needs.

The government of the day was determined to ensure that any new provincial funding would be targeted for specific purposes rather than simply used to increase the value of the BIU (i.e., inflation). One way to control cost increases was to squeeze economies and efficiencies out of the system by ignoring inflation. That, in turn, resulted in improved productivity — a supposed clear "win-win" — a fallacy finally unmasked in Rae's report (Rae, 2005, p. 95). Meanwhile, the Tory's onus on the economy quickly led to direct intervention in the postsecondary sector.

In an era of the "dot-com revolution" anticipated shortages of hi-tech personnel led to representations by industry for greater investment in certain areas. Led by Nortel's John Roth, the industry called for a major increase in the number of computing and electrical engineering graduates — necessary to fuel the research labs and support the hi-tech industries. This investment was deemed to be pivotal to Ontario's future and the government responded with its Access to Opportunities Program (ATOP), setting a goal of doubling the "pipeline" of computing and electrical engineering graduates; several years and a dot-com implosion later, the ironies are obvious.

The government also added other targeted envelopes for specific enrolment increases in professions in the broader public sector (BPS) (teacher education and medicine). For a government committed to market

---

[12]Prior to 1998, all programs that were eligible for government funding were also subject to government tuition policy. Generally, tuition was very similar across programs. Each year government would announce the level of allowable tuition increase. In 1996, 1997, and 1998 the government allowed tuition in all programs to increase, on average, by 10% each year. However, by allowing a maximum increase of 20% in any one program, it became possible to begin introducing tuition differentials by program. The deregulation of certain professional programs and graduate programs in 1998, extended the concept of differential tuition and there are now major differences in tuition by program.

principles (or so it seemed), its foray into centralized human resource planning was a major shift in direction. While one might rationalize the BPS initiatives, since government ultimately had to employ the vast majority of those graduates, the ATOP initiative was central planning at its colossal worst; rather than use an existing well-understood mechanism to implement the initiative (strategic corridor shifts in the corridor parlance), government officials designed their own convoluted, complex arrangement that created enormous amounts of work and continue, to this day, to require separate reporting requirements. The rationale at the time was that the strategic corridor approach was too limiting; government wanted a mechanism to *shift* existing spaces into computing and engineering, rather than *add* new spaces on top of existing enrolments.

The 1998 provincial budget also saw the introduction of what was called the Fair Funding for Universities Grant (FFUG) that was, ostensibly, supposed to address funding inequities among the universities. In effect, over a three-year period, all universities were to move towards the average provincial grant level of the University of Toronto. Of course, since some institutions were above the University of Toronto threshold a number of institutions, including Toronto, received no FFUG funding. Regardless of what the FFUG and ATOP were intended to do, the fact is both initiatives reflected the government's increasing penchant for intervention and the use of what appeared to be arbitrary measures and processes with little (or no) consultation.[13] Moreover, while government could legitimately claim it was adding money to the universities, in fact the funds were distributed in a highly differentiated fashion, thus heightening tensions among the universities.

After 1998 the emphasis shifted to preparing for the "double cohort" and the result was continuing chaos and uncertainty. The announcement of a major commitment for new capital expansion (SuperBuild) ended up tarnished by the absence of any reference to operating funding and an allocation process that was skewed towards the colleges despite the fact that the double cohort, by definition, would have a much greater impact on the university sector. The tuition deregulation of 1998 was slowed

---

[13]The corridor renegotiation of 1989–90 had also identified specific enrolment priorities at the "system level" and concerns were expressed about too much government intervention. The Tory intervention was seen as significantly "worse" because it was regarded as pandering to the interests of big business, the overall funding situation was dire, and it was viewed as a harbinger of things to come.

Ken Snowdon

considerably in 2000 by the imposition of a policy that limited increases in "regulated programs" to 2% per year for five years — a cumulative total of 10% over the period.[14] Programs that had been deemed "cost-recoverable" (e.g., Law, Medicine, Engineering, graduate programs) were exempt from the 2% limits. Nevertheless the sudden change in government policy added to the general turmoil of the period. After introducing Key Performance Indicators to provide more information to prospective university (and college) students, the government decided to tie a performance fund to the indicators. For the first time the government also acknowledged the general increase in enrolment levels (accessibility fund) but accompanied the provision of more funds with what were seen as punitive eligibility conditions.

The government also introduced changes in the postsecondary "market", ostensibly, to allow more competition by introducing a process for more universities (public or private) to operate in the province and by introducing a process to allow the colleges to begin offering applied degrees (Post-secondary Education Choice & Excellence Act 2000). Then, in a misguided attempt to meet the changing entry to practice requirements for Nursing students, the government announced that universities and colleges had to act together and offer joint degree programs. Within a very short time government was establishing yet another mechanism to accelerate the production of nurses. Attempts to get government to recognize the added costs associated with collaborative exercises and the basic underfunding of existing Nursing programs, fell on deaf ears. With the double cohort looming, universities were pressured to make the government initiatives work — endure some short-term pain to demonstrate a willingness to help solve government's problems. The same result occurred in Medicine. As concerns about doctor shortages began to garner attention, government wanted the universities to expand medical enrolments. The five universities with medical schools (McMaster, Ottawa, Queen's, Toronto, and Western) were prepared to expand enrolment but required additional funding beyond that provided through the existing funding formula. Government responded by threatening to change the formula without adding new funds. The universities buckled.

---

[14]Polling results indicated that the "double cohort" was beginning to garner a bit of attention and specific concerns focused on accessibility ("will there be room?") and affordability (tuition increases were drawing more negative press and student protests). The government's change in direction aligned with the polls.

The announcement of a task force to look at efficiencies and effectiveness — the Investing in Students Task Force — was seen, by many, as the final ignominy. Together the preceding government actions, coupled with no provision for general inflation, simply left the university community disheartened and demoralized.[15] To be fair, the Investing in Students Task Force was needed to validate university and college claims about efficiency. Government was not willing to commit additional funding to the double cohort until it was satisfied that universities and colleges were pursuing appropriate efficiencies. However, to the university community it was seen as more evidence of a government trying to duck its double-cohort commitment. As it turned out, the task force's findings were proof positive that additional funding was required. However, once again, rather than rely on existing processes and mechanisms, the government introduced a new process called enrolment target agreements (ETA) to ensure that universities and colleges would, in fact, take additional students if additional funding was made available. The distrust was palpable.

The change in government from Harris to Ernie Eves resulted in a much better working environment for the universities and an apparent genuine desire to address the looming double cohort. Under Eves, additional capital funding was provided, the accessibility fund (renamed the Enrolment Expansion Fund by the Liberals) was augmented, and the first instalment of a $200 million quality fund was implemented.

As the short-lived Eves' era wound down, formula financing was still in evidence, centred on the concept of enrolments but augmented with a number of targeted funds each with its own allocative mechanism. Nevertheless, the basic operating grant — the grant related directly to the corridor formula — constituted about 80% of provincial operating funding.

This brief history of provincial operating grant funding does not do justice to the many machinations associated with government funding over the period. But it helps to illustrate the extent of the changes in the funding mechanisms and funding processes that simply exacerbated the provincial funding picture. To the extent that planning and predictability are important prerequisites to the effective utilization of resources in support of public

---

[15]The punitive nature of government announcements in 2000 were seen, by some, as payback for the fall 1999 universities press release where J. Ibbitson, columnist for *The Globe and Mail*, suggested the universities were trying to "blackmail" the premier (Harris) into more funding. The Harris government took a dim view.

policy one can see the difficulty. The vagaries and vicissitudes of provincial funding policies, and the implementation of those policies, have not helped the situation.[16]

The Federal Presence: "mixed reviews". The federal presence during this latter era also deserves comment. After essentially balancing the federal budget on the backs of the provinces, the federal government began re-investing directly into the postsecondary sector through a variety of funding vehicles beginning in 1997.

The Canada Foundation for Innovation provided major research infrastructure grants. The Canada Research Chairs program was aimed at the recruitment and retention of faculty. Overhead on federal granting council funding focused on the "indirect costs" of federally sponsored research and increases in the federal granting council budgets were aimed at increasing support for basic research. Together those initiatives combined to provide significant sums of funding to the university sector.

At the personal level, new and enhanced tax credits for students helped ease the cost of attending university or college. The Canada Millennium Scholarship Foundation was established to increase accessibility through direct bursary support. In 2002, the Pierre Elliot Trudeau Foundation was established to provide funding support to doctoral students and support to faculty in specific areas. The next year the Canada Graduate Scholarship Program was announced with 4,000 scholarships to be available by 2006.

In Ontario, the federal programs incensed the Tories. After slashing transfer payments the federal government was seen as spending money that rightfully belonged to the provinces and, to rub salt into the wound, many of the federal programs came with conditions that required provincial contributions. The fact that some university presidents heaped praise on these federal initiatives did little to improve the overall working relationship during the Harris years. Provincial bureaucrats looked for ways

---

[16]An illustration of the problems of government continually altering policies and directions concerns international students. In the mid-1990s government withdrew provincial funding for international students. Institutions were allowed, however, to charge tuition at "cost-recoverable" levels and keep the revenue. Within a few years, institutions were told to place greater emphasis on double cohort students and thus many reduced their international enrolment. More recently, universities (and colleges) are being urged to be more entrepreneurial and seek out international students.

to turn the federal monies to their own advantage. The Millennium Scholarship program was used to trim provincial student assistance expenditures and establish new provincial scholarships. The Indirect Costs program led some to believe that provincial officials saw little need to provide inflationary funds to universities. By 2002/03, as documented in the Rae Report (p. 96) the federal contribution to the postsecondary sector had changed markedly: transfers to the province had dropped by almost 50% in real terms since 1992/93; transfers to individuals in the form of tax credits, research grants (to the universities), bursaries and student loans had increased markedly. The advent of the new scholarship awards announced in 2002 and 2003 will continue the shift in federal funding.

The federal programs had another major impact: differentiation. The decision to use "research" as the focus of the federal investment in universities resulted in quite different allocation results than if the funds had flowed through the province and been distributed through the operating grants mechanism. Institutions with a research presence, as measured by their share of federal granting council funding, benefited markedly. Strength in research led to more strength in research with all of the associated costs and benefits. Between 1995 and 2004 a major transformation occurred; by virtue of federal funding initiatives involving billions of dollars, a very small set of Canadian institutions emerged as the clear research leaders.[17]

Setting the context for the Rae Review. With the election of a Liberal government in late 2003, and a deteriorating fiscal situation, the stage was quickly set for another review. The new government found itself committed to the funding requirements of the double cohort and an election promise to freeze tuition and offset the loss of tuition income that had already been factored into institutional budgets. Budget 2004 announced the launch of the Rae Review.

As the Rae Review started the existing funding arrangements included the basic operating grant allocated on the basis of the corridor formula, targeted enrolment envelopes for specific enrolment increases (teacher

---

[17]In fact, the allocation mechanism is a bit more complicated than just shares of federal grants. Under the guise of "capacity building" the actual allocation mechanisms for CRCs and indirect costs have specific provisions to ensure smaller universities receive a share of the funding; it's Canadian, eh.

Table 1: Total Operating Grants — 2004/05 ($000s)

Grant Category	2004/05 ($000s)	% Dist.
Basic Operating Grant	1,868,400.7	81
Enrolment Expansion	81,438.4	4
Quality Fund	74,597.5	3
Performance Fund	23,160.0	1
Research Overhead Fund	27,751.8	1
Mission-related Fund	46,140.2	2
Tuition Freeze Compensation	41,700.0	2
Access to Opportunities	53,027.0	2
Institution Specific	55,386.7	2
All Other	22,792.7	1
Total Operating Grants	**2,294,395.0**	**100**

Source: Hon. Mary Anne Chambers, *Memorandum to Executive Heads of Provincially-Assisted Universities, 2004–05 University Operating Grants Allocations and 2004–05 Accountability and Funding Agreements*, August 19, 2004. Table 1.

education, Medicine, Nursing), the Access to Opportunities Program, an enrolment expansion fund (Access) for general growth and the double cohort, a quality fund, a performance fund, a research overhead fund allocated on the basis of shares of tri-council funding, a host of special purpose funds and mission-related specific grants.

On the tuition front, the Liberals froze tuition for 2004/05 and 2005/06. The Rae Review is intended to help shape government policy for the 2006/07 year. Prior to the freeze tuition for the majority of students (undergraduates) had been limited to about 2% per year since the announcement in 2000. In the case of the "cost-recoverable" professional programs, as noted earlier, institutions had full discretion in setting fees, subject to ensuring student assistance provisions were in place. At the graduate level, the government policy was the same as that for the preceding professional programs — institutions were free to set the tuition level providing student assistance provisions were in place.

Federally, the university sector had come to rely on the various federal programs, yet it was unclear about the long-term nature of the commitments. The CFI, CRC, and Millennium Scholarship programs, for example, were funded with one-time allocations and had time limits associated with the duration of the programs. Moreover, it was becoming increasingly difficult for the new provincial government to determine how it should respond to the federal initiatives. A program like the Canada Graduate Scholarship Program, for example, was consistent with the need to encourage students to pursue graduate studies. Yet increases in graduate enrolment led to demands for more provincial operating funds.

Finally, another major funding source, private sector donations, were coming off another year of relatively "flat" performance. While private donations had increased markedly in the latter part of the 1990s, fuelled by government "matching" programs, an expansion of fundraising operations, and a robust stock market, the experience of the last few years reflected different economic conditions and stories about "donor fatigue".

As Rae assumed the mantle of yet another review of postsecondary education he faced a more complex financial situation than his prede-cessors. In total, absolute funding had never been greater. Yet it seemed apparent that more funds would have to be invested to keep up with burgeoning enrolments. Regardless of where the funds came from, the fiscal climate demanded the prudent use of all resources and evidence that new investments would yield tangible results; hence the need for a look at accountability.

Accountability

The postsecondary sector has been subject to calls for more accountability for many years. Despite the fact that the enabling legislation for each institution was set by government and requires some specific reporting on a regular basis, the universities have been swept up in the government's penchant for accountability, subject to increasing scrutiny by the provincial auditor since the late 1980s, and subject to an increasing reporting burden. Table 2 chronicles the major provincial government accountability initiatives of most relevance to the universities.

Table 2: Summary of Provincial Accountability Initiatives

- 1988 to 1991: Inspection audits of three universities by provincial auditor
- 1991 to 1993: Task Force on University Accountability (Broadhurst Report)
- 1995: Ontario Financial Review Commission
- 1997: Ontario Budget — discussion of Public Sector Accountability Act
- 1999: Report of the provincial auditor on university accountability
- 2000–2001: COU-Ministry Task Force on the Provincial Auditor's Report
- 2001: Public Sector Accountability Act (proposed)
- 2003: Multi-year Base Funding Accountability Framework (pending)
- 2003–2004: Bill 18, Expanding the powers of the provincial auditor (value-for-money audits)

The Broadhurst Report had major implications for universities because it was aimed specifically at university accountability. As such, the report provided a detailed accountability framework for universities and, at least initially, all institutions moved to implement various recommendations. The Broadhurst Report highlighted the important role of the Governing Boards and argued that the boards were (or needed to become) the locus for accountability in the university sector.

Interestingly, while the universities themselves were being asked to be more accountable, the fact is the ministry was being asked as well. The Provincial Auditor's Report on the Ontario Student Assistance Program identified weaknesses in the ministry's accountability mechanisms and led to more formal auditing requirements. The provincial auditor's report, *Ministry Accountability Framework for University Funding*, concluded that it was difficult to determine how well the university system was meeting provincial needs and achieving postsecondary objectives. That report included specific recommendations in a host of areas including university governance and accountability processes, measuring and reporting program quality, access, monitoring the financial health of universities, university performance reporting, and funding university education. The university community responded by developing a more prescriptive accountability framework and articulating a set of "shared goals" (Council of Ontario

Universities, 2003b) with the Ministry of Training, Colleges and Universities as follows:

- All appropriately qualified Ontario students will have access to a place in an Ontario university.
- No student will be denied access to the program of his or her choice for financial reasons.
- The education received by Ontario university students will be the best in Canada and on par with that offered in the best public universities worldwide.
- Research support will enable Ontario's faculty and students to add valuable knowledge and produce economic and societal benefits to all Ontario residents such that the province secures a reputation for excellence in both its scientific/medical and its humanities/social sciences research.
- The physical environment of Ontario universities will be safe, up-to-date, accessible to those with special needs, and will enhance the learning effectiveness of each student's educational experience.

As of Spring 2005 there had been no formal response by the ministry.

Leading up to the Rae Review there had been successive initiatives to introduce greater accountability into the public sector and the universities were swept along with the tide. The efforts of the university community to demonstrate that their own houses were in order and jointly develop a workable framework with government essentially fell on deaf ears. The government has focused on ensuring that all ministries have appropriate accountability mechanisms in place. One result of increased ministry interest in accountability is increased reporting and that is the legacy to date as evidenced by the following partial list of reporting requirements. But is it accountability?

At the time of the Rae Review, Ontario's universities had been actively engaged in improving their own *internal* accountability mechanisms and major strides had been made at many institutions in implementing the recommendations of the Broadhurst Report. It is entirely possible that the missions, visions, and goals of 19 individual Ontario universities would, collectively, sum to the needs and objectives of the province. Nevertheless, the provincial auditor's report, *Ministry Accountability Framework for University Funding*, suggested strongly that the government needed to be more prescriptive in setting objectives and holding the universities accountable. The stage was set for a review.

Table 3: Existing Reporting Requirements to the Ministry

1. Enrolment Target Agreements (ETAs) and all related reporting
2. Audited financial statements
3. Audited enrolment reports
4. Capital Plan Investment reports
5. Major Capital Support Program reports
6. Facility Renewal Program reports
7. Ontario Student Opportunity Trust Fund (OSOTF) Status Report
8. Access to Opportunity Program (ATOP) reports
9. Ontario Graduate Scholarships in Science and Technology (OGSST) reports
10. Bilingualism Grants reports
11. Tuition Fee Set Aside Reports
12. Tuition Fee Survey
13. Tuition Fee Monitoring Reports
14. Accessibility Funding for Students with Disabilities reports
15. Quality Assurance Fund reports
16. Audited OSAP Compliance Reports (every three years)
17. Reports on Special Purpose Grants to individual universities, including:
    - Aboriginal Education and Training Strategy Program reports
    - Educ-Action reports
    - Interpreters Fund Reports
    - Women's Campus Safety Grant Reports
    - Nursing: Compressed/Masters Expansion/Collaboration reports
    - Reports on Programs of French as a Minority Language
18. Graduate Survey (for the KPIs)
19. USIS reporting (enrolment reporting, November, February, May, July)
20. New Program Approval submissions

Source: Council of Ontario Universities (2004b, Appendix B).

Ontario: A Leader in Learning

Overview of the Rae Report

Faced with a somewhat daunting task, Bob Rae established three over-arching goals to focus his recommendations: (i) *Great Education*; (ii) *Opportunities for More People*; and (iii) *A Secure Future for Higher Education*. It is in the strategies for the latter goal that he outlines a proposed revenue framework, a regulatory framework for tuition increases, and the importance of multi-year plans as a linchpin for accountability. The preceding strategies are intended to support the very first recommendation of the Rae Report, as follows:

> Legislate a mission for Ontario as a Leader in Learning, founded on: access for all qualified students to higher education, excellence and demonstrable quality in teaching and research; institutional autonomy within a public system; and the mutual responsibility of government, institutions and students. (p. 39)

The strong commitment to legislation is a key component of Rae's overall plan. It is clear he has come to the conclusion that without a strong sense of mission and a set of goals (what are you trying to do?) it is extraordinarily difficult to figure out how to do it and muster the resources to make it happen. Moreover, how can you be held accountable? To have the mission enshrined in legislation reinforces the reality of the goals, the public nature of the postsecondary system and, hopefully, government's commitment to provide the requisite funding. Securing the funding, allocating it in support of those goals, and being more visibly accountable are the key elements associated with the goal of *A Secure Future for Higher Education*. In Rae's estimation it begins with the revenue framework.

> Establish a new framework that provides sustainable revenues for institutions, in which the key funding partners — the provincial and federal governments, institutions, students — each contribute in a responsible and predictable manner. Obtain a commitment from the federal government to become a full funding partner in supporting base operations and priorities for labour market training and immigration, apprenticeship, research and graduate education in a predictable and sustained way. Invest a total of at least $1.3 billion in new provincial base funding to institutions by 2007–08. This investment would focus on quality improvements and results, fund enrolment growth and ensure that all eligible students are

properly funded. It should include funding to institutions that covers: higher costs incurred by institutions serving significant numbers of students that require additional services, the high cost of providing clinical education and the base adjustment for revenues lost as a result of the tuition freeze. Allocate provincial funding through a new transparent formula comprised of core funding for basic operations and strategic investment envelopes tied to results, and applied to both colleges and universities. By 2007–08, the per-student revenue base of Ontario's colleges and universities should be at least comparable to other provinces. This would require at least $1.5 billion in new revenues to institutions. The "stretch target" over the long term should be to bring the per-student revenue base up to the level of public institutions in peer North American jurisdictions. This would require approximately $2.2 billion more in revenues to the institutions than they receive today. (p. 92)

The proposed revenue framework speaks to four points: (i) expected contributions from all partners; (ii) a major investment of provincial funds to be allocated through a formula that includes core funding and strategic investment envelopes (see Table 4); (iii) specific reference to a minimum and a "stretch" target for per-student revenue with timelines; and (iv) the importance of responsible and predictable funding. Together those points combine to provide enormous potential to address many challenges facing Ontario's universities.

By establishing a provincial investment figure of $1.3 billion and a minimum and stretch target for per-student funding of $1.5 billion to $2.2 billion Rae is clearly indicating that all partners will have to contribute. The province may be the largest investor, but to "close the gap" requires more than just the provincial investment.

The emphasis is on responsible and predictable funding as key elements of the framework because it speaks to the importance of governments (federal and provincial) providing sufficient funding to meet the true cost requirements (including inflation) associated with the first goal: to make Ontario a leader in learning. Moreover it reinforces the importance and value of planning to the achievement of goals. As we saw previously, the chaos of the last decade or so has not been conducive to planning nor the efficient use of resources. Interestingly, Rae is specifically recommending additional funding in one particular discipline area, health sciences, thus apparently validating the Nursing and Medicine funding concerns noted earlier.

Table 4: Rae Review: Specific Funding Recommendations

(additional annual funding required from province by 2007–08, $million)

		Investments in Colleges and Universities	Support for Students and Other Expenditures
Quality			
Academic Renewal/Student Experience, includes adjustments for		700	
- Previously unfunded enrolment growth			
- Keeping up with cost increases			
Council on Higher Education			8
International			10
	Subtotal	**700**	**18**
Participation and Access			
Enrolment growth		88	
Expand graduate education		180	
Aboriginal		13	2
Francophone		20	
Persons with disabilities		15	
Northern and rural		20	
First generation		5	
Web portal			1
	Subtotal	**341**	**3**
Affordability			
Tuition stabilization		115	
Medical and clinical		100	
New tuition grant (net new expenditure)			193
Supplemental loans to parents			21
Ontario Student Opportunity Trust Fund			50
New Ontario Learning Bond			36
	Subtotal	**215**	**300**
	Total	**1256**	**321**
Capital			
Facility renewal		200	
New facilities		300	
Equipment		40	
	Total	**540**	

In terms of specifics, it appears the predictability aspects of the revenue framework flow through to the allocation of funding to institutions.

> Provincial grants would be allocated as "core funding" and supplemented by a number of clearly defined and well-targeted envelopes for graduate students (universities), apprenticeship (colleges), broader public sector programs such as medicine, nursing, education, mission-specific institutional requirements, and access priorities such as students from Aboriginal and francophone backgrounds, and students with disabilities. (p. 97)

With respect to the core funding envelope, Rae endorses the existing university "corridor formula" and indicates that it should be extended to the college sector. With respect to targeted envelopes, specific mention is made to consolidate the number of envelopes "to link funding with results achieved" and in the case of the graduate funding envelope there is specific reference for incentives "to increase enrolment and improve time-to-completion". Formulaic allocation mechanisms can be designed to include the "predictability" factor into the equation.

The report also speaks to a key characteristic of the funding formula in Ontario universities: "The allocation of provincial operating grants will be equitable — students in similar programs at different institutions will receive similar funding from government" (p. 97).

Rae is explicitly acknowledging that the *government grant* will be similar but the other major component of funding, tuition, may be quite different in similar programs at different institutions. As noted previously, at one time the funding formula ensured the government grant and tuition income per student were essentially the same in similar programs at different institutions. The deregulation in the Common Sense Revolution effectively broke the link.

Tuition, which is dealt with as a separate recommendation, would be set by institutions subject to a regulatory framework "enshrined in legislation". The framework would "ensure that future increases are predictable, transparent and affordable ... institutions would be responsible for supporting low-income students and students in need to cover fees in excess of $6,000 per year" (p. 99). The tuition regulation appears to apply to direct-entry undergraduate programs, only implying that all other programs would, by definition, be deregulated.

Together, the proposed revenue framework and the proposed tuition regulation provide the vehicles to secure the additional funding to close the gap. Further, the framework incorporates a few key principles that should guide the actual allocation of funds to individual institutions.

The final piece of *A Secure Future for Higher Education* involves the use of multi-year plans to provide the required accountability in a visible fashion. Those multi-year plans would include:

- the mission and program focus of the institution;
- enrolment targets, commitments to access, and tuition guarantees;
- planned improvements in quality of programming and the student experience;
- transferability of credits and areas of collaboration with other institutions;
- revenue requirements and how they will be met through provincial transfers, tuition, and other sources; and
- the results and measures that will be used to demonstrate progress against the multi-year commitments.

"These plans should be informed by the work of the Council on Higher Education. A Standing Committee of the Legislature should conduct periodic reviews of individual institutions' multi-year plans and performance" (p. 104).

If the new legislative framework is intended to answer the question "what are you trying to do?" do the proposals in the revenue framework and tuition regulation provide the means? And does the proposal for multi-year plans provide the appropriate accountability mechanism to feel confident about the ends? The devil, as they say, is in the details.

Assessing the Rae Approach

Recommended Funding Levels. Before turning to the specific mechanisms inherent in the framework, it is important to assess the *adequacy* of the overall level of required funding identified in the Rae Report. As noted in the previous table, the total sums to almost $2.1 billion and applies to both colleges and universities: $1.3 billion for operating, $300 million for student assistance, and $540 million for capital. Of the $1.3 billion for operating costs, a major portion appears to be earmarked to "close the funding gap" between Ontario and other jurisdictions.

The use of other jurisdictions as benchmarks appears, on the surface, to be a reasonable way to determine whether the level of current funding is more or less adequate. The fact is, however, benchmark comparisons are only as good as the chosen benchmarks. There are considerable structural differences in the provincial higher education regimes across Canada, and major differences between Ontario and public systems in the United States.

From the Rae Report itself it is difficult to determine the exact funding comparisons that were made. In the case of the universities the "gap" is identified as about $1,000 per student in 2002 or approximately $300 million ($380 million by 2004/05), but no details are provided.[18] There are, in fact, many reasons to suspect that the identified funding gap with other provinces is actually higher (Snowdon, 2005). Moreover, there is little in the way of comparative analysis that indicates levels of access and quality elsewhere and so it is not clear what the funding benchmarks actually mean. Does greater provincial investment in other provinces result in greater access and/or quality?

Interestingly, given the *Leader in Learning* moniker, there is little reference to the benchmark leaders, but rather a focus on the benchmark average (or less). The "stretch" target is actually a "stretch" to the average funding levels. One could argue that a *Leader in Learning* should be heading towards the leading benchmarks. In the case of the comparison with public universities in the United States, that funding gap alone is identified as $1.8 billion (p. 94). The fact that Rae is suggesting that only $380 million is needed to close the gap with universities in other Canadian provinces illustrates the serious funding disadvantage faced by all Canadian universities relative to public funding levels in the United States.

There were, of course, other options to arrive at an estimate of the funding required to improve access and quality. It would have been possible to construct a number of assessments of university (and college) finances and arrive at funding requirements based on assumptions about increased enrolments, improving student to faculty ratios, meeting space standards, improving library collections, and improving student services. It may be that the Postsecondary Review Secretariat did that kind of modelling, but it is not evident in the report.

This review of the adequacy of the proposed funding is not intended to be a criticism of Bob Rae nor the Postsecondary Review Secretariat. Meaningful jurisdictional comparisons are very difficult and fraught with pitfalls. There is considerably more work to do to arrive at good comparisons to inform public policy decisions. In that regard, the report's recommendation

---

[18]The figure of $1,000 per FTE is cited in Riddell (2003, p. 28).

about the establishment of a Council on Higher Education, and the research role of such a council, is welcome and perhaps will fill the need identified in the Smith Report (1996) to improve the "publicly available information on postsecondary education and research" and produce a "regular report on the comparative strengths and weaknesses of Ontario's system relative to those in other jurisdictions" (p. 10).

In the meantime, there is no question that the proposed infusion of new public funding will make a difference. Will it be enough to make Ontario a *Leader* in Learning? That is difficult to judge at this juncture. What we can do though, is assess the mechanisms that Rae is proposing against the stated goals of access for all qualified students, excellence and demonstrable quality in teaching and research, institutional autonomy within a public system, and the mutual responsibility of government, institutions, and students.

Access. The legacy of the Robarts era carries over into Rae's views on access. He refers to education as the "bedrock of opportunity" and his proposals are aimed at encouraging greater participation. In that regard he takes the Robarts policy a step further — Ontario needs to ensure Ontarians are provided with the opportunity to pursue postsecondary education. Access to postsecondary has moved beyond providing a place to those who wish to pursue such an opportunity; it is now an imperative and government must be proactive in encouraging greater participation (and funding access in a "responsible" manner).

Access is a function of a number of factors including affordability, outreach, and capacity. Rae appears to have dealt with the first two issues in a fair, balanced way. Through the use of an upfront grants system for low-income students and targeted funding for underrepresented groups the proposals should have a positive impact. In the case of middle-income families he recommends easier access to loans and reduced loan costs. It appears he believes tuition is reasonably affordable for the majority of students and cites evidence on private returns to help justify future increases.

Rae acknowledges the importance of increasing capacity to deal with access and he recognizes that core operating funding as well as increased physical infrastructure must be included in the equation. In the case of core operating funding it appears he endorses a continuation of providing average grant funding for projected enrolment increases, although he stresses the importance of increasing participation for all underrepresented

Ken Snowdon

groups. Special supplementary grants would then be used for specific groups as defined — aboriginal, francophone, persons with disabilities, northern and rural, and first generation. The *existing* array of funding envelopes includes specific reference to programs for aboriginal people and persons with disabilities. Additional funding would be added to enhance existing programs. In the case of persons with disabilities he recommends the distribution of funds be based on the actual number of students with disabilities rather than a *prorata* share based on total enrolment — an eminently reasonable proposition that will be tested when trying to determine how many persons with disabilities are actually on campus.

With respect to the other specific groups, different mechanisms are proposed to improve access including special outreach programs. Improvements in participation can be measured and Rae's emphasis on setting participation targets and monitoring progress towards those targets will help focus more attention on access issues and access strategies.

The proposed increases in capital funding for facilities renewal and new construction are positive developments and important contributors to improving access. Facilities renewal funding helps ensure existing facilities can be used in the most effective way and also helps to fund the physical infrastructure needs of persons with disabilities. Currently, the facilities renewal monies in the university sector are allocated on a formula basis using imputed space requirements — a reasonably sound and fair system that recognizes the legitimacy of reasonable space standards. Each institution receives a share of the facilities renewal funding based on its imputed space requirements using a methodology that involves inputs (numbers of students, numbers of faculty) and specific space standards for varying types of space (classroom, laboratories, offices, library, etc.). The allocation of the facilities renewal funding provides a direct link to a specific set of inputs and, along with something called the facilities condition index (FCI), provides a systematic way of measuring the impact of the facilities renewal investment on the condition of the physical infrastructure. All institutions have invested in the appropriate software and personnel to collect the required information and it has become part of on-going operations. The actual space standards, originally established in the 1970s, are reviewed on a regular basis, updated as required and are generally seen as a reasonable measure of space requirements, although there has been concern expressed about the need to adjust the standards for research space.[19]

Capital funding for *new* construction has always been somewhat of a contentious issue given the politics associated with capital decisions; politicians like to be able to cut ribbons and such projects provide some economic benefit to the community. The most recent provincial experience in the university and college sector was the SuperBuild program (now called Public Infrastructure Renewal Projects) associated with enrolment growth and the double cohort.

The SuperBuild initiative led to the greatest investment in the post-secondary sector since the "baby-boom" expansion of the 1960s. SuperBuild involved a competition for provincial funds with criteria as follows (Ministry of Training, Colleges and Universities, 1999):

- Allowance for enrolment growth: how many additional students would be accommodated?
- Private and non-provincial government funding contributions: how much funding would be provided by "other" sources?
- Student demand: was there evidence that the university had sufficient demand or would have sufficient demand to fully utilize the facility? and
- Community-Regional impact: how would the project benefit the long-term economic strength of the community and region?

Individual institutions could add other considerations such as the current state of facilities (quality and quantity), but it was clear that the main determinants would be the preceding four items. More importantly, given the government's general views about encouraging private sector contributions and maximizing the use of available funds, there was a general sense that the first two criteria would carry added weight in the evaluation.

The initial results of the competition were a boon to some and a bane to others. The apparent overemphasis on the "cost per space borne by government" led to the college sector being awarded a disproportionate share of the spaces. The attempt to use a supposed competitive rational allocation device fell into disarray in the face of political realities and the realization that significant student demand was going to be in the university

---

[19]For a detailed review of the space standards see COU (2003a).

sector. By the time the SuperBuild allocations were completed there were actually three major allocations, Spring 2000, Fall 2002, and Spring 2003, and it was evident that some basic planning assumptions had gone awry. As the students voted with their feet, it became crystal clear that government had allocated too much capacity to the college sector and too little to the university sector. Moreover, the assumption that institutions would be able to raise private monies to help meet the overall capital requirements gave way to the reality of fundraising shortfalls. At many institutions, operating budgets had to absorb the added burden of capital financing. Buildings were built and the double cohort was accommodated. Would a more formulaic approach have yielded a better result?

Bob Rae makes no recommendation about the actual mechanics of the capital allocation he is proposing ($300 million for colleges and universities combined) other than to suggest that it should be tied to enrolment plans and that private sector contributions, while welcome, should not be factored into the allocation process. The reference to enrolment plans could be read as suggesting the funding should be based on planned enrolment increases. That, of course, implies an emphasis on accessibility. At this time, however, virtually every university in the province has less space than the space formula dictates and some institutions are below 50% of the calculated entitlement. To the extent there is support for formula funding one could argue that all, or most, of the capital funding should be allocated on a formulaic basis. In fact, if government were to move in that direction the facilities renewal funds and the new construction funds could be pooled and allocated formulaically. Institutions would then be able to make sensible trade-offs about whether to renovate space (renewal) or replace it with new space. Moreover, the predictability associated with the formula financing would enhance the use of those monies significantly.

Excellence and Demonstrable Quality in Teaching and Research. Given the overall level of new provincial investment recommended by Rae, it is evident that he is relying on two other factors to realize this goal: tuition increases and an accountability framework that involves multi-year plans with institutional commitments to measurable quality improvements.

In the case of tuition, the report is very clear:

> Greater tuition fee variation will promote institutional and programmatic differentiation, by accommodating the unique revenue needs associated

with different approaches to program delivery, student services and quality enhancements. (p. 102)

Internal resource allocation policies within the institution have a major role to play in fostering "excellence and demonstrable quality in teaching and research". Too great a reliance on "funding follows the student" can lead to greater balkanization, "haves" and "have-not" faculties and schools, and unintended results. Institutions will have to be clear about their own internal resource-allocation policies. That, in turn, should lead to greater attention actually being paid to costs and the differentiated nature of costs across an institution.

Will increased tuition lead to improved quality? Certainly the additional revenue from tuition, along with the other revenue identified by Rae, will help provide the necessary wherewithal to have a demonstrable impact on the inputs that we tend to equate with "quality" — more faculty, reduced student/faculty ratios, better facilities, updated equipment, etc. Tuition increases, however, must not be seen as a substitute for provincial grant increases if there is to be quality improvement; witness the lessons of the mid- to late 90s.

In thinking about the impact of increased funding on "excellence and demonstrable quality" it is important to recognize that there are a number of competing claims for all new resources. A very large portion of institutional costs is driven by compensation adjustments for faculty and staff. In 2003/04, for example, salary and benefit payments totalled over $3 billion and represented about 75% of operating expenditures.[20] Each 1% increase in compensation is about $30 million. Faculty compensation represents about 60% of the total. That reality has two key elements: the impact of differentiated tuition on compensation levels; and the pivotal role that compensation plays in excellence and demonstrable quality.

In the case of the first issue, there is evidence that faculty in programs with differentiated tuition (e.g., Business, Engineering, Law) have gained relative to faculty in programs where tuition is regulated. Market considerations are often cited to justify higher starting salaries for junior faculty. That in turn leads to claims from existing faculty for anomaly adjustments or other compensation arrangements. To the extent that one

---

[20]Interestingly, the next largest expense was scholarships and bursaries at $323 million (COU. Committee of Finance Officers, 2005, p. 36, Table 6: Expense/ Operating).

Ken Snowdon

faculty can more readily pay (through differentiated tuition income) there is greater likelihood that the local faculty ability to pay may supplant true market considerations. Institutions will need to carefully consider the best way to ensure that true "market" considerations are determining hiring salaries and requests for anomaly adjustments or special compensation dispensation. On the one hand the collective bargaining process acts as a check on the range of ongoing compensation practices within an institution. That is to say there is a propensity to treat the professoriate as a single entity, all doing the same job regardless of the specific market considerations. However, at the point of hire, the collective bargaining process is not in play and there can be wide variations in the salaries of new hires.

One might argue that in a true market, students and government (as the two principal funders) should be able to exercise some influence on faculty compensation increases. Governments, one might argue, can influence the overall ability to finance compensation increases through the level of operating grant. If institutions decide to award compensation adjustments in excess of the revenue provided by government, the consequences involve internal resource-allocation trade-offs (e.g., increased class sizes, using more part-time faculty, reducing allocations for library acquisitions, reducing faculty or staff complements). Supposedly, the process for approving the compensation increase would weigh the consequences and determine what is in the best interests of the institution. It is less clear how students paying differentiated tuition influence decisions about compensation increases.

Bob Rae understands the importance of compensation on "excellence and demonstrable quality". On the one hand it is important to have the best faculty available and those faculty deserve, and will command, a reasonable salary. Moreover they should have some reasonable assurance that their individual salary will increase in real terms over their career. On the other hand, faculty compensation is such a large part of the overall expenditure equation that providing annual increases can leave little for improvements in student to faculty ratios, library acquisitions, learning technologies and basic infrastructure. Rae speaks directly to the point in his opening essay:

> There needs to be a candid discussion — and consequent decisions — to ensure that new money does not simply translate into much higher, across-the-board salary increases. Pay systems should be sufficiently flexible that real merit and outstanding performance can be appropriately rewarded. Student contact, mentoring and teaching excellence have to be strong components of compensation incentives. If substantial amounts of new

money are simply swallowed by the existing system, without improvements in the quality of the student experience, nothing much will have been achieved. Both governments and students would rightfully feel that an opportunity had been squandered. It is well within human will and ingenuity to ensure that new money means better and more tangible results. (p. 17)

Rae makes a careful distinction between across-the-board salary increases and pay systems that incorporate or allow merit provisions and the rewarding of outstanding performance. In that regard his exhortation is similar to recommendation 16 of the Report of the Advisory Panel on Future Directions for Postsecondary Education (Smith Panel, 1996):

We recommend that governing boards of colleges and universities ensure that a high proportion of compensation increases is awarded in recognition of excellence in teaching and, in the case of universities, of research performance, and that without becoming involved in individual cases, governing boards ensure that appropriate processes are in place to assess and reward performance. (p. 11)

Bob Rae knows that compensation systems can have an impact on quality and he is also cognizant of the pitfalls (internal and external) of having a disproportionate amount of the recommended new funding "swallowed by the existing system". The proposed solution to this rather delicate problem is imbedded in the concept of multi-year plans. As envisaged by Rae,

Each institution will start by setting out, in consultation with students, government and the community, goals and strategies to meet its mission, contribute to the province's accessibility targets and enhance educational quality. These discussions will drive the establishment of each institution's multi-year revenue requirements. (p. 95)

The process of arriving at and publishing these plans will supposedly keep all the parties and interests "honest". A transparent process — involving exploring ways to realize cost savings — will convince all of the parties of the need for prudent use of resources, provide the justification for compensation increases and the rationale for any tuition increases. The added suggestion to have institutions report to a standing committee of the legislature could be seen as yet another factor that would help with transparency and thus yield mutually satisfactory results.

Will it work? As Rae discovered during his Social Contract experiment, collective bargaining in the public sector is characterized by entitlements and an interesting disregard for fiscal realities (Rae, 1997, ch. 13). Rational arguments and full disclosure of all information *may* improve the process but there is little evidence the result will change.

What are the options? Perhaps the proposed Council on Higher Education will be able to provide the necessary analysis and publish appropriate reports that will help ensure all decisionmakers are fully apprised of the compensation arrangements at each institution. Better information may lead to better decisions. Perhaps government could use moral suasion to ensure that funds are directed to quality improvements. Perhaps government targets the funds for quality improvements and uses the new powers of the provincial auditor to ensure the funds are used for specified purposes. Each of those options involves more government intervention than the university community is likely to want, although the provincial auditor, with new found powers, will soon be knocking on the universities' doors in any case. If government begins to fund inflation — as recommended by Rae — that may help to ensure that more of the *new* funding is available for quality improvements.

Another option is to formally place this issue squarely in the hands of university governance: Senates and Governing Boards. One of the puzzling omissions in the Rae Report is the lack of any reference to governance given the important role that both Senates and boards could (and should) play in the quest for improved access, excellence, and demonstrable quality in teaching and research, and in reinforcing the importance of institutional autonomy. Both bodies have representation from various communities in the institution. The board represents the one entity on campus with fiduciary responsibility that has representation from all of the "communities" — students, faculty, staff, government, alumni, interested citizens, and the administration. Governance structures in the institution should be responsible for developing and approving multi-year plans, monitoring progress, and ensuring that the institution is paying attention to "excellence and demonstrable quality". In that process governance bodies will have to become more familiar with compensation issues and key policies that influence compensation levels and the inherent resource allocation trade-offs.

At the same time the selection, monitoring and publication of quality indicators may help provide a decision-making environment where various factors affecting quality are taken into consideration. In fact, Rae is quite explicit about one quality indicator in particular — the use of surveys of student engagement. The National Survey of Student Engagement (NSSE) and the Community College Survey of Student Engagement (CCSSE) are regarded as steps in the right direction to begin collecting information that provides more insight into the factors that may influence student engagement. As such, over time, the results may help inform internal resource-allocation decisions and a variety of institutional practices and policies.

Finally, to reinforce the importance of this particular goal — excellence and demonstrable quality in teaching and research — the report calls for the proposed Council on Higher Education to take a lead role in the development of a quality assurance framework that would include both quantitative and qualitative measures at the system level and institutional level.

Institutional Autonomy within a Public System. The proposal for legislated frameworks and multi-year plans with public reporting requirements will be seen by some in the university community as a threat to institutional autonomy. Will government have more to say about the programs an institution offers, its planned level of enrolment, the use of resources, and admission standards? Government already has processes in place to approve programs for government funding, set first-year enrolment targets for each institution and targets for some specific program areas. While the government does not stray into institutional admission standards, it has established a minimum admission standard for government funding eligibility. Students must meet that minimum threshold or the institution is not allowed to claim the student for government funding.

There is evidence from the past of government's willingness to exercise greater control, especially if access is seen as being compromised. However, the proposals in the Rae Report may actually provide greater, or at least maintain current, levels of institutional autonomy.[21] Institutions will have the opportunity to "make the case" as individual institutions, focusing on their own mission with goals that are set at the institutional level.

---

[21]The one disturbing part of Rae's multi-year plan is the reference to including all sources of revenue in the plan and the potential for government to therefore factor private giving and investment income into the overall funding equation. Those monies have been differentiating characteristics for some institutions and at one time were often cited as the "margin of excellence". Any explicit attempt by government to factor those funds, in a negative fashion, into institutional or system allocations will have a dampening effect on private giving.

Similar exercises in Alberta and British Columbia as well as the short-lived Performance Contract exercise in Quebec appear to be workable.

But, let's be clear. The sum of the institutional goals must be consistent with *accessibility, affordability,* and *quality* goals of government. To the extent that the legislated framework helps define the goals for the province, and ensures a funding commitment commensurate with the achievement of those goals, the university sector should be racing to embrace the proposal. The lack of a clear set of government goals on those three issues has allowed successive governments to skimp on funding and not be held accountable to Ontarians. The lack of public reporting to the legislature has meant that postsecondary issues have not been given the attention they deserve.

Mutual responsibility of government, institutions, and students. It is clear that Rae believes in the idea of mutual responsibility and his recommendations reflect that belief. There is a "leap of faith" in his prescription of how these players interact and there is a view that each of the players — government, institutions, and students — actually can act as single entities bound together in the common cause for an accessible, affordable, quality-based higher education system. Again, the process of developing, negotiating, and implementing the multi-year plan becomes the vehicle to rationalize the competing interests. The reference to mutual responsibility is important. How it will actually translate at the institutional level is a matter that institutions should be carefully considering because it will impact on governance and decision-making processes. Earlier comments about the perils and pitfalls of the Social Contract may be applicable.

Rae also expects more from the federal government, specifically:

> Financial support through the CST for postsecondary education needs to be restored and increased in the future to keep up with inflation and enrolment increases.... The Federal government should also establish a separate fund to help colleges and universities pay for needed equipment and campus improvements. It should be allocated among provinces on an equal per capita basis. (p. 96)

It is far beyond the scope of this paper to delve into the intricacies of federal-provincial financing.[22] However, Rae's views are quite clear about the federal role. He sees the cut in transfers and the subsequent reinvestment in targeted programs as a destabilizing influence that is not in the best interests of Ontario. Therefore, in his view, the restoration of the CST would help provide the wherewithal to fund an accessible, affordable, and quality system in Ontario. Whether the restoration of the CST should supplant the other funding programs of the federal government (i.e., indirect costs) is an issue left untouched. While one could make a good case for leaving those programs outside any discussion of a restored CST, one could also make a good case for wrapping the funding into the CST. The implications for individual institutions, assuming the funds flowed through to the university sector, are significant.

If the federal government is to have a responsibility role, as suggested by Rae, it is interesting that there is no reference to federal involvement in the development of multi-year plans. Yet, it is recognized that the federal fiscal contribution in research, student assistance and, increasingly, core operations (CRCs and indirect costs) is significant.

Reflections on quality and differentiation. Do the Rae Report funding recommendations establish a framework for improved quality and differentiation? As noted earlier, the overall level of investment will help with quality improvements. To the extent that the allocation mechanisms adopted by government ensure a "level playing field" the competitive nature of universities will help reinforce the importance of quality. As David Smith noted in his seminal piece on quality:

> Universities compete and should compete. They compete for the best faculty, the best students, the most funds, and the best learning environment. For all such attributes, "best" and "most" are defined by the nature of the institution and its mission, but there are varying degrees of overlap among institutions that strengthen competitive incentives. (p. 33)

At the same time Smith also pointed to the importance of collaboration in defining quality:

---

[22]For an interesting insightful review of federal-provincial interactions in the postsecondary sector see Cameron (2005).

Quality also requires a reasonable degree of collaboration among universities.... This collaboration should be based on the more effective use of resources that can be achieved through the combination of teaching, research and administrative matters. (p. 33)

Smith's insights provide a valuable guide for assessing Rae's funding recommendations. Do the recommendations hamper competition? Do they encourage collaboration? For the most part the funding recommendations are neutral and, given Rae's penchant for maintaining the corridor system, the largest component of the new investment may in fact be allocated in a way that reinforces "the level playing field". The exception seems to be the proposed funding associated with the expansion of graduate education where, in addition to increased enrolment, he includes reference to incentives to improve time-to-completion as a potential criterion for the allocation of monies — thus perhaps straying into the murky area of performance funding. The pitfalls of performance indicators and performance funding are well-known (Smith, 2000; Lang, 2005) and there is little need to review them here. It is clear from experiences elsewhere, and the Key Performance Indicator experience in Ontario, that performance funding has little to do with encouraging quality.

The conventional view of Ontario universities, it seems, is that there should be more differentiation — program differentiation and quality differentiation. In fact, there is considerable differentiation in programming and a wide range of institutional mandates.[23] What may be seen as duplication by some (too many Faculties of Education, for example) is actually a reflection of a provincial system that recognizes the importance of geographic accessibility and the realities of program delivery. In the case of Education, for example, students need hands-on learning in the classroom — a reality that is best accommodated by having Faculties of Education located across the province. Further, while on the surface all Faculties of Education may look the same, there are degrees of special-ization and disciplinary focus that are only evident to those who actually take time to explore program offerings in some detail.

In terms of quality differentiation, governments have demonstrated over time that they have great difficulty dealing with the pressures associated with differential funding. It is extraordinarily difficult for the government

---

[23]The Rae Report actually acknowledges that there is considerable progam differentiation and it is one factor that contributes to the difficulties with credit transfer (p. 42).

of the day to admit that it provides more, or less, funding to a certain kind of student at one institution versus another institution. On what grounds would government justify the differential funding? Student marks? More importantly, there are different definitions of quality as noted in a recent Canadian Policy Research Network paper (Finnie and Usher, 2005).

From time to time governments have tinkered with the idea of performance-based funding or even implemented some performance-based elements. But for the most part those funds represent a small fraction of the available funding and have little to do with differentiation on the basis of excellence and quality. In Canada, the granting councils operate, for the most part, on a merit-based scheme that awards individuals (or institutions) on the basis of grant competitions. Those awards can result in significant funding differences at the institutional level. The fact that the federal government has used the distribution of those awards to determine allocations for other funds has already reinforced funding differentiation. Whether it has reinforced quality differentiation depends on definitions of quality.

Rae's funding tool for differentiation is, in fact, tuition. He recognizes the inherent difficulty of government allocating funds on a differential basis and, perhaps more importantly, he suggests that in a mass education system the government's first priority should be to provide access to a quality "system". The real value of the public investment in higher education, the public good, emanates from the provision of a quality education for as many students as possible. However, freedom to set tuition, within certain constraints, is seen as a vehicle to encourage program differentiation and, perhaps, higher quality in select programs. Certainly the provision of additional funds provides the potential for higher quality and program differentiation; but it is not automatic.

Summing Up

The funding and accountability recommendations in *Ontario: A Leader in Learning* are intended to improve access, affordability and quality of higher education in the province. Will they? His key recommendations on a clear set of goals enshrined in legislation, more public investment in core operations, a new up-front grant system for students, and an accountability regime focused on multi-year plans with measurable outcomes, have the potential to help address years of inadequate funding, have a positive impact on the learning environment, improve access, and raise the profile of higher education in Ontario. From a funding perspective, the proposed infusion of new monies, providing there is adequate inflation protection, will provide sufficient funding to allow for greater access and should allow for improved quality inputs — more faculty, more staff, better facilities, expanded facilities, etc. As noted earlier, the funding level is likely not high enough to make Ontario a *Leader* in Learning, but it is a good start.

Rae's endorsement of the "corridor system" for allocating resources is a positive outcome and would appear to reinforce the concept of formula financing. If funded adequately, formula financing provides an allocation mechanism that "levels the playing field" — a necessary pre-condition to a competitive environment. That general mechanism has served Ontario well and government should adopt the basic concept of formula allocations (as opposed to funding competitions) in the various funding envelopes. Equitable funding — that is students in similar programs at different institutions will receive similar funding — should not be seen as a rejection of quality considerations but rather as a necessary part of establishing the competitive framework. Ontario's universities are competitive and yet, at the same time, work together on a host of program delivery and service delivery initiatives. Rae has recognized the intrinsic and real value of that competitive/collaborative balance and judged it to be about right, with the exception, perhaps, of the need for more collaborative efforts between colleges and universities.

Rae has assessed the more market-oriented funding approach of the early Common Sense Revolution and he is not prepared to tread very far down that path. He clearly recognizes the public good/private good arguments and has tried to develop a plan that speaks to current political realities which, in turn, are influenced by the polls of the day. Ontarians want an affordable, accessible postsecondary system. For the most part that system is viewed as government's responsibility. Over the longer term some of Rae's proposals, such as greater incentives for saving, better information for prospective students, better student assistance for low-income families, and more student assistance in postsecondary institutions, may lead to tuition playing an even greater role in quality and program differentiation. In the short term, however, an infusion of provincial funds is necessary; the simpler the allocation mechanisms, the better. After 15 years of turmoil one could argue Ontario's universities (and colleges) need a period of adequate funding with predictable funding levels and stable funding mechanisms so they can, in fact, focus on providing a quality learning experience.

Finally, the advent of multi-year plans is seen as *the* mechanism for keeping government and institutions honest. In return for greater public investment institutions will have to commit to deliverables that are consistent with government's access, affordability, and quality objectives. In return, government commits to greater public investment. The existence of "deliverables" explicitly addresses accountability and the incorporation of measures into the multi-year plans provides the opportunity for regular monitoring. The multi-year time frame is also conducive to improved planning and improved predictability, two important ingredients in the effective and efficient utilization of resources.

At the same time, the multi-year plan commitment to deliverables (and government funding) may remove the incentive for government to constantly tinker with funding mechanisms. As noted earlier, government intervention through funding allocations and funding mechanisms can have quite negative effects. By putting the onus on the importance of a stable funding mechanism like the corridor model, coupled with "responsible" funding from government, Rae underscores appreciation of the importance of predictable funding and the benefits that can accrue in an environment where the focus is on goals and deliverables rather than just the means.

That focus on goals and deliverables will worry academe, and it should. The negotiation of multi-year plans with government has inherent risks and may well lead to a Faustian bargain where institutional autonomy withers away in return for greater government funding. To counter that worry, Ontario's universities, each of them, need to have a clear vision of the future and a clear sense of purpose, and be prepared to argue, as a system, that the sum of the parts is, in fact, greater than the whole; that a set of institutions can compete and at the same time collaborate in an efficient and effective manner; that self-regulation wherever possible is preferable to government regulation; and that their own governance systems are up to the challenge of realizing the Rae vision.

Rae's prescription for the postsecondary sector offers the potential for improvements in access, affordability, and quality. At one level he has kept it simple: What are you trying to do? (goals); What do you need to get there? (means — strategies, tools, resources); and How would you know that you are making progress? (ends — indicators, public reporting, deliverables, accountability). At another level, the devil is in the details, and the details rest with government.

Ken Snowdon

References

Advisory Panel on Future Directions for Postsecondary Education. 1996. *Excellence, Accessibility, Responsibility: Report*, Toronto: Ministry of Education and Training, Government of Ontario.

Cameron, D. 2005. "Post-secondary Education and Research: Whither Canadian Federalism?" in F. Iaccobucci and C. Tuohy (eds.), *Taking Public Universities Seriously*. Toronto: University of Toronto Press.

Cameron, D. and D.M. Royce. 1996. "Prologue to Change: An Abbreviated History of Public Policy and Postsecondary Education in Ontario", *Appendix B: Background Paper*, in *Report of the Advisory Panel on the Future Directions for Postsecondary Education*, December.

Commission to the Association of Universities and Colleges of Canada (Bladen Commission). 1965. *Financing Higher Education in Canada*. Toronto: University of Toronto Press.

Corry, J.A. 1970. *Farewell the Ivory Tower*. Montreal: McGill-Queen's University Press.

Council of Ontario Universities. 2003a. *Inventory of Physical Facilities of Ontario Universities, 2001-02*. Toronto: Council of Ontario Universities.

_____. 2003b. *Shared Goals and Building Blocks*. Toronto: COU.

_____. 2004a. *A History of the Funding Formula in Ontario*. Draft unpublished, August.

_____. 2004b. *Proposed University Accountability Framework*. Submitted by COU to the Postsecondary Review, November 15.

_____. Committee on Enrolment, Statistics, Projections and Analysis. 2001. *Enrolment Review: Report of the Committee on Enrolment Statistics, Projections and Analysis*. Toronto: COU.

_____. Committee of Finance Officers. 2005. *Financial Report of Ontario Universities, 2003-04*. Toronto: COU.

Darling A.L., M.D. England, D.W. Lang and R. Lopers-Sweetman. 1989. "Autonomy and Control: A University Funding Formula as an Instrument of Public Policy", *Higher Education* 18(5).

Finnie, R. and A. Usher. 2005. *Measuring the Quality of Post-secondary Education: Concepts, Current Practices and a Strategic Plan*. Ottawa: Canadian Policy Research Networks.

Ibbitson, J. 1997. *Promised Land: Inside the Mike Harris Revolution*. Toronto: Prentice-Hall.

Johnstone, D.B. 1998. *The Financing and Management of Higher Education: A Status Report on Worldwide Reforms*. Washington, DC: World Bank.

Jones, G.A. 2005. *Complex Intersections: Ontario Universities and Governments*, in F. Iacobucci and C. Tuohy (eds.), *Taking Public Universities Seriously*. Toronto: University of Toronto Press.

Lang, D.W. 2005. "The Political Economy of Performance Funding", in F. Iacobucci and C. Tuohy (eds.), *Taking Public Universities Seriously*. Toronto: University of Toronto Press.

Leslie, P.M. 1980. *Canadian Universities, 1980 and Beyond*. AUCC Policy Studies No. 3. Association of Universities and Colleges of Canada.

Ministry of Training, Colleges and Universities. 1999. *SuperBuild Growth Fund for Postsecondary Education*, October.

_____. Universities Branch. 2004. *The Ontario Operating Funds Distribution Manual, 2003-04*, December.

Provincial Auditor. 2001. *Accountability Framework for University Funding: Follow-up*. Toronto: Ministry of Training, Colleges and Universities.

Rae, B. 1997. *From Protest to Power: Personal Reflections on a Life in Politics*. Toronto: Penguin Books.

Rae, The Honourable Bob (Advisor to the Premier and the Minister of Training, Colleges and Universities). 2005. *Ontario: A Leader in Learning. Report and Recommendations*. Toronto: Postsecondary Review Secretariate.

Riddell, W.C. 2003. *The Role of Government in Post-Secondary Education in Ontario*. Background Paper for the Panel on the Role of Government in Ontario, October.

Smith, D.C. 2000. *How will I know if There is Quality?: Report on Quality Indicators and Quality Enhancement in Universities: Issues and Experiences*. Toronto: Council of Ontario Universities.

Snowdon, K. 2004. *Applicant Data in Canada: Another Perspective on Access*. Montreal: Canada Millennium Scholarship Foundation.

_____. 2005. "'Muddy' Data: University Financing in Canada", in C.M. Beach, R.W. Boadway and R.M. McInnis (eds.), *Higher Education in Canada*. Kingston: John Deutsch Institute, Queen's University.

Trow, M. 1974. "Problems in the Transition from Elite to Mass Higher Education", in *Policies for Higher Education*. Paris: OECD.

The Rae Report and the Public Finance of Postsecondary Education

Robin Boadway

Introduction

My purpose is to view the proposals of the Rae Report from the perspective of the economics of public finance. Public finance is the study of government involvement in the economy. In its normative form, it begins with the fundamental question of the rationale for government intervention, and from there studies the options available for achieving those objectives, taking account of features of the economy or of government itself that constrain government policy. From a public finance perspective, a notable aspect of the report is that, despite its inclusion of a number of proposals for improving the quality, accessibility, and financial soundness of the higher education sector in Ontario, there is an absence of discussion of the underlying rationale for given forms of public intervention. The proposals also tend to be exhortative in nature, with bold calls for improved delivery of postsecondary education services, legislation to set the framework, and institutions to advise and monitor, but relatively little detail about how policies might be designed to get there. This paper largely explores the latter.

In applying the principles of public finance to postsecondary education (PSE), it is useful to begin with some caveats that limit the extent to which universally accepted prescriptions can be inferred. There is a distinct lack of consensus about the policy prescriptions arising from study of public finance for at least three key reasons. First, value judgements are necessarily involved in establishing the objectives of government policy since the latter inevitably involves redistributive consequences. Reasonable persons can disagree on the weight to put on the nature of equity objectives and how to weight them against efficiency. Second, the trade-off between equity and efficiency, and even the need for government intervention, depends on an understanding of how the market economy works, and how it responds to policy. We are not well informed about that, and different persons will have different prior presumptions. Finally, one's preferences for government intervention depend upon one's view of the benevolence of government. To the extent that one regards government as self-seeking and serving its own or special interests, one will be less willing to rely on government policy to achieve desired ends. These sources of disagreement apply to the study of the role of government in PSE. We should be aware of them in what follows.

The Rae Report takes a somewhat more limited perspective. Rather than beginning with these basic questions about the role of government that would lead to a questioning of the manner in which government should intervene in PSE, it takes as given the existing system and asks how it can be improved. It does this partly through admonition and the setting of legislative and institutional frameworks, and partly through securing more financing from existing stakeholders using existing mechanisms in an equitable manner. There are no sweeping changes in institutions or in methods of finance, nor any in-depth exploration of the arguments that should determine the shares and modes of financing for various stakeholders, including students and their families, governments, and the private sector.

This is reflected in the three broad objectives in the Rae Report, which deal with quality, accessibility, and financial security. The first objective — *Great Education* — is to improve the quality of education by legislating a mission for PSE that would emphasize accessibility to all qualified students, excellence in teaching and research, institutional autonomy and joint responsibility of government, the institutions, and the students. This would be facilitated by setting up a new Council on Higher Education, by investing in teaching excellence, and by the setting of quality standards.

The second objective — *Opportunities for More People* — focuses on accessibility. Emphasis would be on informing and attracting all qualified students, especially those from under-represented segments of the population. This would be supported by enhanced student grant and loan programs directed to those students in need, and by ensuring that the teaching and capital requirements are in place to accommodate the growth in students.

The third objective — *A Secure Future for Higher Education* — is to ensure that PSE institutions have the resources to meet these commitments to excellence and accessibility. The province is asked to provide enough new funding to bring Ontario's per student funding up to the national average by 2007–2008 and up to North American standards in the long run. The federal government is also expected to increase its funding by assuming responsibility for certain activities. A regulatory framework for tuition would also be established, with universities responsible for assisting students in need for fees in excess of $6,000 per year. Finally, provincial funding should be based on multi-year plans rather than being on a budget-year basis.

As mentioned, despite the changes in legislative and governing frameworks that may serve to codify missions and goals, and despite the emphasis on attracting more under-represented, qualified students, the approach to financing is basically incremental. The resources of PSE institutions should be enhanced by more of the same. Both governments and students should contribute more to existing institutions, and student assistance programs should be enhanced so that accessibility is not denied. Presumably, there is much that the federal government could do to address the accessibility issue. Indeed, it is hard to imagine the problem of PSE funding being fully addressed without taking a coordinated approach to student assistance using both federal and provincial assistance programs and tax incentives. However, since the report is aimed at provincial policies, detailed recommendations for federal government intervention are absent. More generally, fundamental questions about the role of government and the rationale for the existing mix of policies are not posed.

The Rationale for Government Intervention

To put the Rae Report into perspective, it is useful to go back to first principles. Suppose we do not feel constrained to take the present institutional and financing setup as given. What then might public finance principles suggest about the role of government in the PSE sector? A useful approach to take, following the standard paradigm, is to think of government as a default option, only needed if the private sector fails to meet society's needs.

PSE could, in principle, be provided completely by the private sector. If so, there are a number of possible sources of market failure that might justify government intervention on either efficiency or equity grounds.

Credit Constraints. Pursuing PSE involves a significant investment by students of both time and resources, especially if the price charged must cover the full institutional costs. Unless potential students have access to private wealth, they will be forced to borrow to finance the investment. Although this might be mitigated by an income tax system that allowed interest deductibility and had refundable tax credits, the student would have to rely heavily on borrowing from financial institutions. There are reasons why such institutions might be reluctant to lend sufficient amounts of money to cover all costs. Most important, they may not be willing to lend against future earnings except at high interest costs. This could deter students from less well-off families from investing in PSE. Not only would this be inefficient, it might be viewed as inequitable, both from the point of view of unequal outcomes and from that of equality of opportunity (discussed further below).

Risk and Information Problems Facing Students. Related to this, there is considerable risk associated with investing in PSE from the point of view of the student, whether or not financing is secured. Part of the risk results from imperfect information about one's skills or chances of success in higher education. As well, part arises from not being able to predict the future rewards, both earnings and chances of employment, that different courses of study will yield. Despite the fact that students learn something in secondary school about their own skills and aptitudes, much risk remains, and it is difficult to insure against it. Insurance companies would not be willing to offer full insurance because of standard problems of moral hazard and adverse selection, and students would end up bearing the risk. This too would lead to inefficiencies, and would discourage potential students from investing in PSE, especially those with limited resources who have less ability to self-insure.

Risk and Information Problems Facing PSE Institutions. PSE institutions themselves may be subject to problems of risk and information. They may not be perfectly informed about the quality of students that they admit. As well, they may not be able to predict the demand for various types of degrees and qualifications. As well, these institutions face so-called agency problems of information internally. They may not be able to monitor well the performance of their faculty and other employees. And, there may be important incentive problems involved that affect the quality of their output. For example, the profit motive may encourage them to be overly generous in their assignment of grades, at least in the short run.

Failure of Competition in the PSE Sector. More generally, there may be problems arising from the competitive provision of PSE services by private institutions. The efficiency of private markets requires the free entry and exit of firms, as well as full information and products that are relatively homogeneous. The market for PSE services is likely to be inefficient on various grounds. Institutions will have economies of scale, which precludes the marginal cost pricing needed to support socially efficient outcomes. Services offered are differentiated, resulting in monopolistic competition rather than perfect competition. Competition for students may result in a stratification of students by quality into different institutions. This may not be efficient to the extent that peer-group effects are particularly important in determining the success of less-able students or those from disadvantaged backgrounds.

Externalities of PSE. A standard argument for government intervention in PSE is that there are externalities associated with aspects of the higher education process. Research activities, which are natural features of universities and complements of teaching, yield knowledge whose benefits cannot (and should not) be appropriated by those understanding them. There may well be more subtle externalities resulting from the acquisition of skills and knowledge by students that are passed on to others in society by human interaction of various sorts. PSE institutions also perform services that benefit local communities, such as mounting cultural events, providing local leaders, offering educated commentary on local issues, and establishing museums.

Equity Objectives and PSE. Finally, but no less important, PSE may be a uniquely important form of public service from an equity perspective. There are a couple of dimensions to the equity argument. One is simply that access to PSE by disadvantaged persons can lead to less inequality both across individuals and across different types of communities. PSE can be seen as a policy instrument that complements other redistributive policies, such as the tax-transfer system, in reducing inequality.

Perhaps more important is the role of PSE as a device for pursuing equality of opportunity. Section 36(1) of the Constitution Act, 1982 commits the federal and provincial governments to "promoting equal opportunities for the well-being of Canadians". The concept of equality of opportunity has different interpretations, and the public finance literature so far provides only limited guidance. One concept is that persons of given personal characteristics should have comparable opportunities to exploit those characteristics. In particular, they should not be penalized according to how they exercise them, nor should they be compensated for exercising them in ways that may leave them apparently disadvantaged. Thus, a person of given skill should not be compensated for choosing to live a life of leisure relative to one of diligence. At the same time persons should be compensated for differences in skills since they have no control over that. This view of equality of opportunity as allowing every person to be responsible for their own free choices is the one found in the well-known work of Roemer (1998). From the point of view of PSE, it suggests that persons ought to be able to pursue higher education based solely on their educational skills rather than their ability to pay.

A somewhat more far-reaching notion of equality of opportunity, and one that has particular resonance for PSE, is that opportunities should be made more equal regardless of initial skill levels. Thus, if persons are endowed with different skills that would enable them to perform differently in the economy, skills should be made more equal by a proactive PSE policy that devotes more resources to the low-skilled than to the high-skilled, subject to the extra costs associated with upgrading the skills of low- versus high-skilled persons. The analogue in the elementary and secondary education system is devoting relatively more attention to slower learners. This is a somewhat more controversial notion of equality of opportunity, and one that poses special difficulties for PSE, where attainment may be more skill-dependent than for school education. Moreover, it is not at all clear how lower-skilled persons could be targeted in the PSE system. It does, however, have implications for the quantity of PSE places supplied. To the extent that one believes in this stronger version of equality of opportunity, one would opt for higher participation rates and more resources to ensure that students can succeed.

Robin Boadway

Implications for Government Policy

These concerns constitute potentially serious problems with relying solely on the private sector for the delivery of PSE. It is therefore not surprising that governments are heavily involved in PSE in all Organisation for Economic Co-operation and Development (OECD) countries. It is worth staying with principles for the moment and asking what kinds of policy interventions might be used to address the above problems, or more generally what sorts of information is needed to devise well-founded policy prescriptions. Unfortunately, many of the same problems that preclude private provision from being efficient and equitable also constrain public policy, especially those involving information imperfections. Because of that, policy prescriptions are bound to be imprecise, and well-informed persons are likely to disagree. Nonetheless, it is useful to identify the sources of imprecision and disagreement.

We can distinguish between policies that apply to students and those that apply to PSE institutions.

Policies Applying to Students

There are several interrelated problems that policies applying to students need to address. They have been already referred to above. Pursuing PSE is an investment that involves both finance and time. It involves risk that is hard to insure against. It involves imperfect information. There may be externalities associated with PSE that involve benefits to third parties. And, equity effects of the sorts mentioned above may be regarded as important.

Suppose we set aside equity effects for the moment, and focus on efficiency alone. The first question is: What should be the cost of PSE borne by the student? This in itself is a difficult question to answer since it involves many considerations, most of which are not easily quantified. Presumably, the cost to the institution of providing the education will be a determinant, but there are two main difficulties with identifying that cost. First, the cost of educating a student should be separated from the costs of research activity in the PSE institution. Second, if there are returns to scale in university education (e.g., administrative and other overheads), the marginal cost of education will be lower than the average cost. On efficiency grounds this would suggest pricing below average cost. Both of these factors are difficult to measure, but both point in the direction of tuition well below the per student cost of running PSE institutions. When one adds to this the fact that there may be externalities associated with higher education — which are also non-measurable — the proportion of the costs of education borne by the student would be even lower. The student costs of education will also involve forgone earnings, which the student necessarily bears. This will have some implications for the tax treatment of PSE to which we return below.

Suppose that the student's share of costs has been decided, and this is reflected in tuition and ancillary fees. The matter does not end there because of the financing and risk costs that students must face. Combining tuition fees with forgone earnings implies that the financing costs to a student can be substantial. Those students who must borrow to cover the costs may find the borrowing costs to be quite high for reasons mentioned earlier. Moreover, there is considerable uncertainty about the outcome of PSE reflecting both the risk of success itself and imperfect information about employment prospects in the future. To the extent that this risk is insurable, instruments can be devised for doing so. The broadest form of insurance would be one that encompasses all students nationwide. Thus, an income-contingent loan program that is actuarially fair would be suitable. (A graduate tax program accompanied by an up-front grant would accomplish the same thing.) Here, the income-contingency reflects insurance rather than income-distribution considerations. Actuarial fairness would take account of the possibility of defaults. Of course, there are many design issues in constructing such a program, which space precludes us from discussing. The key point is that, if the costs of education to be borne by students already take account of arguments for subsidization, loan schemes should be self-financing.

On efficiency grounds, an income-contingent loan program would address both the issues of risk and borrowing difficulties. To the extent that individuals did not need to borrow, they would not need to participate in the scheme. By not participating, however, they would forgo the risk-pooling advantages of such a scheme. Of course, there is a possibility that persons may choose not to participate if they know that they are lower risk. If this adverse selection problem is perceived to be significant, one might consider making participation compulsory (much like automobile and health insurance may be mandatory partly to avoid adverse selection issues). As well, there may be moral hazard problems in the sense that persons may choose to have lower incomes in the future to avoid high repayment rates. In this case, some co-insurance scheme could be built into the system. It is not clear that either of these problems is likely to be significant in practice.

Note that, as well as there being no requirement for individuals to participate in income-contingent loan schemes, there is no need to limit participation by income-testing. All persons should be allowed to participate regardless of their means or those of their parents.

What then are the arguments for grants to needy students, given the above discussion? That is, why should different students pay different costs for the same thing? One might argue that, if the income tax-transfer system were designed effectively, all redistribution would be done through it and there should be no need to subsidize particular services. This is especially so in the case of PSE, which gives rise to higher expected earnings in the future. If a well-designed income-contingent loan system is in place, and the general level of tuition already takes account of externalities of education, why should the average taxpayer subsidize students to obtain a higher education that yields above average earnings in the future? This is not an easy question to answer, and it is not one that the Rae Report has shed light on.

A couple of possible arguments for grants to students from low-income families come to mind. One is that, while the tax-transfer system is reasonably effective at reducing inequalities arising from differences in one's labour and capital income, it is not very effective at reducing inequalities arising from differences in inherited wealth. There is not an effective system of inheritance taxation, and there is not an effective system of reducing inequalities arising from in-kind and inter-vivos inter-generational transfers. One of the most important forms of intergenerational transfers takes the form of parental support for PSE. Differential treatment of students according to the income of their parents is thus an indirect way of reducing inequalities from this source.

This argument is reinforced by equality of opportunity considerations. Two persons of comparable skills ought to be given the same opportunities to use those skills. In the absence of a perfect tax on intergenerational transfers, those from better-off families will have greater opportunities (and incentives) to pursue PSE. Of course, once the PSE is completed, earnings attributed to it will be subject to the redistributive income tax. How persuasive this argument is as a basis for grants to needy students is a matter of judgement. What the discussion seems to make clear is that such grants have their rationale in the shortcomings of the tax-transfer system to achieve all of society's desired equity objectives.

Finally, it is worth considering how all this interacts with the income tax system. Some of the elements mentioned above could be integrated with the income tax system. An income-contingent loan or graduate tax program should be operated through the income tax system, given that income is reported there. The case of grants for needy students is more difficult. In principle, it could be operated as a refundable tax credit. However, there are a couple of reasons why that may not be completely satisfactory. One is that refundable tax credits typically come with a lag, whereas PSE grants are needed up-front. Another is that the measure of need used for grants will differ from what one reports on one's income tax form. For example, parental income will be needed if one takes the equality of opportunity arguments seriously. This would make it more complicated to use the income tax system, though not impossible. The enormous advantage of the income tax system is that it would be relatively low cost to use. But, the need for timely grants may preclude using it.

If the grants are to be separately administered, it may be preferable to do so using a government agency rather than the PSE institutions themselves. The latter are not particularly well-equipped to evaluate student need, even though they are now called upon to do so. They may not have access to the kind of reliable information required to implement a system of need-based grants fairly, and their incentives may not align well with society's objectives. For example, they may give extra weight to the quality of the student along with their need when deciding on grant allocations.

More generally, how should PSE investments be treated by the income tax system? If human capital investment were to be treated like other assets whose returns are taxed, stringent measurement requirements would be necessary. Human capital would have to be costed like other assets, based on deductions for interest on financing and economic depreciation. This, of course, is practically impossible. Instead, human capital investment is treated on a cash-flow basis, implying that it is effectively tax-sheltered like pension contributions and housing.[1] It seems reasonable to assume that this is the only feasible way of treating human capital investment, implying that it already has a tax advantage over investment in financial assets and

---

[1]Cash-flow tax treatment means that all expenses, including investment ones, are deductible when they are incurred, and all returns are taxed when they are received. In the case of PSE, cash-flow treatment means both tuition costs and forgone earnings are deductible when incurred, which is the case, and increments in future earnings are fully taxed. This is the same way in which pension and Registered Retirement Savings Plans (RRSP) savings are treated.

Robin Boadway

personal businesses. If all taxes were proportional, there would be no tax incentives affecting human capital accumulation one way or the other, whereas the accumulation of assets whose returns are taxed would be discouraged.

There are, however, some things in the tax system that detract from pure cash-flow treatment. One is that not all costs of education are deductible when they are incurred. For example, tuition fees are not fully deductible for tax purposes. As well, to the extent that the tax system is progressive, the tax liabilities on future earnings are taxed at a higher rate than the tax savings on forgone earnings during the period of education. Both of these things imply that the tax system discourages human capital investment. These anomalies could be undone by the following measures. Tuition and ancillary costs paid to PSE institutions could be fully deducted from income for tax purposes. Moreover, the tax savings on these would have to be fully refundable, which is certainly feasible given the existing technology of tax administration. And, there would have to be an income-averaging system available to PSE students so that the effective tax rate paid on their future income does not exceed the effective tax rate that applies when they are attending educational institutions. If such a system were in place, the current system of tuition and education credits could be eliminated. Note that their purpose is partly to offset the costs of higher education in a way that is more beneficial to low-income earners. However, if low-income persons are being taken care of using other measures, the tax system ought to be designed with efficiency objectives in mind. A rationalized system would treat need with one policy instrument dedicated to the purpose, rather than attempting to take some account of need in other policy instruments.

Policies Applying to Institutions

The manner in which government policies should affect PSE institutions is equally problematic. If the standard principles of market competition applied, one could argue in favour of a fully decentralized approach where institutions are free to produce whatever services they prefer, and set their own prices for these services. Moreover, there would be free entry and exit into the sector. Of course, government financial support would be needed to the extent that the activities of the institutions yield benefits that are not appropriated, but this support would be otherwise unconditional.

In fact, as we have observed, the standard competitive model is not applicable to the university sector. There are likely to be significant economies of scale in provision. The services being provided by PSE institutions are diverse and differ from institution to institution, implying that monopolistic competition exists. Problems of asymmetric information abound both within the institutions and in their dealings with students. Students are not likely to be well informed about the value of the service they are acquiring at a PSE institution. The competition for students, while healthy from the point of view of imposing some discipline on institutions, can also give rise to adverse outcomes. In particular, there is an incentive for institutions to skim off the best students, who have peer-group effects on their colleagues. There are also benefits from coordination among institutions in areas like student admissions. Once one brings in issues of redistributive equity and equality of opportunity, the role of the competitive decentralized model is even more problematic. How can one ensure that needy students with limited means can be induced to attend, and be accepted at, PSE institutions?

Despite these problems with competition in PSE, some elements of the competitive model are undoubtedly valuable. Competition among institutions can be healthy if it induces them to provide their services more efficiently. Competition from parallel private institutions that have freely entered the sector would have a similar benefit. How much decentralization of decision-making should exist in the PSE sector? And, should competition from private institutions be allowed? These are all difficult problems, but ones that must at least be recognized in any fundamental review of higher education. One cannot simply legislate and admonish the achievement of quality. But at the same time, it is not clear how government oversight can induce PSE institutions to operate cost effectively, produce high quality students, and meet society's equality of opportunity objectives.

Suppose we set aside these issues of quality control and institutional management and focus on resource-allocation matters. Unfortunately, it is very difficult to make categorical arguments for the way in which PSE institutions ought to be financed. A consensus view about the role of these institutions has not been developed, and we are far from perfectly informed about the balance between decentralized, competitive decision-making and controlled, cooperative decision-making in this sector. The Rae Report has not really been able to engage in the kind of analysis to inform us of these key issues. Given this state of affairs, one way to proceed is to ask what sorts of questions would have to be addressed in order to have a rational policy for financing PSE institutions. The list might include the following.

Number of Students. The overriding issue that must first be addressed is how many students ought to receive higher education. This is a difficult question, even in principle. Hypothetically, one could imagine a cost-benefit calculation in which the social benefits from education are compared with the costs. However, given that the benefits are so amorphous, this would be difficult to execute. It might be argued that at least private benefits should exceed the costs of education, and the former can be estimated using rate-of-return estimates based on the effect of higher education on earnings, which is a common enough procedure. However, even this is problematic, even if one accepts that the main private benefit of PSE is higher earnings. The problem with these calculations is that they measure the average rate of return on education, and not the marginal one, that is, the benefit to the marginal student. Since marginal benefits are likely to be significantly lower than average benefits, these calculations overestimate the return to the least able students. Moreover, there is likely to be considerable uncertainty about the rate of return. How this uncertainty should be taken into account in rate-of-return calculations is not at all clear.

Things become more complicated when equality-of-opportunity issues are factored into the calculation. If equality of opportunity simply means ensuring that equally qualified students should have an equal chance of success, the optimal cut-off ability of admitted students should not be affected. Instead, the allocation of spaces should be changed in favour of needier students, and this can be accomplished by appropriate student financing schemes of the sort already discussed. On the other hand, if equality of opportunity means that more resources ought to be devoted to improving the success of less qualified students, this implies a lowering of the cut-off for student admissions.

These are all difficult issues to grapple with quantitatively, but simply posing them is of some value. One might suppose that an indicator of an appropriate cut-off is the rate of success in completing higher education. There is some merit in this argument. But since success rates are endogenous, one could not put too much emphasis on them as indicators of the optimal supply of spaces in PSE institutions.

Type and Number of Institutions. The target number of students obviously affects the type and number of PSE institutions. However, even given the number of students, there are a number of policy decisions that need to be addressed. These involve the size and mix of universities. The ideal size for a given university depends on a number of factors. There are presumably economies of scale, at least within given faculties. These economies of scale are not just with respect to teaching services, but also involve research, in terms of both research costs and critical masses of faculty in related areas. To the extent that these are exploited, there could be a small number of large universities. On the other hand, it could be argued that size detracts from the benefits to students, both size per se and the implications of size for average distance from home.

Institutions can also vary in terms of the services they offer. As in the current system, there could be some specialization in programs offered. In the case of universities, some could be full service and offer a wide range of professional and/or graduate programs. Others could specialize in, say, undergraduate liberal arts education. As well, the mix between research and teaching could vary from institution to institution. Institutions could also vary significantly in terms of the quality or ability of students that they attract. These issues affect the manner in which financing is allocated among universities.

More generally, institutions could include both public institutions and private ones, with the latter presumably relying less on public funds for their operation. Of course, the possibility of allowing private institutions to compete with public ones may be moot, given the difficulties that new entrants would face. The track record elsewhere of new private universities starting up in a pre-existing public system is not great. Perhaps the only feasible alternative would be the privatization of existing public institutions. While this may well serve to inject some more competition into the system, it would also create a more stratified system, where students are segmented by ability to pay rather than ability to learn. Alternatively, one might seek to create more competition among existing public institutions by giving them more autonomy in all aspects of decision-making, including the setting of fees.

These questions about the optimal size and mix of institutions are ones that need to be asked. They are important for deciding on the allocation of operating funds, as well as longer-term decisions like capital spending, faculty renewal, and basic questions about changing the nature of existing institutions (e.g., creating more degree-granting options in community colleges, increasing the number of graduate programs) or adding new ones. They are also important for determining the extent to which institutions ought to be free to decide for themselves issues like tuition, student numbers, and programs to offer.

Robin Boadway

By and large, the Rae Report put relatively little emphasis on these questions. That is understandable given the limited amount of time and resources available to them. Perhaps the intention was that they would become part of the mandate of the proposed Council of Higher Education. If so, that is a worthy objective.

Proportion of Costs to be Publicly Funded. PSE institutions can obtain funding from various sources, including various levels of government, private donors, students, and the private sector. From the point of view of the government role, there are two main issues. One is what the overall share of government funding should be, and the other is what should be the source of marginal or residual financing to PSE institutions.

The first question involves judgements about the importance of externalities in PSE education, the share of research versus teaching in institutional costs, the consequences of scale economies for pricing, and the need for funding to achieve equity goals. All of these are difficult to quantify, but at least they provide a conceptual framework for framing the issues.

The second question goes to the heart of the extent of autonomy of the institutions. If residual financing requirements are in the hands of the institutions themselves, there will be an incentive for cost-effective management and also for innovation in service delivery. These seem like strong arguments for requiring institutions to have the discretion for raising marginal sources of revenue on their own, whether these are from tuition changes, attracting more students, or seeking more funds from alumni and industry. The possible downsides result from some of the alleged adverse consequences of competing for students and funding. For example, if institutions really do have some monopoly power as a result of the differentiated products they provide and the restrictions on entry of possible competitors, it could be argued that tuition will be excessive, and the values of institutional competition exaggerated. As well, there may be adverse consequences for accessibility of needy students, at least to the extent that student financing is inadequate.

To the extent that one regards these concerns to be serious ones, they could be tempered by some restrictions on the discretion to set fees, and a close relation between fees and access to funding by needy students. The Rae Report in fact argues for such measures, although neither the details nor the rationale were clearly spelled out.

Funding Formula. The manner in which public funding is allocated to institutions also raises a number of conceptual problems. There are two broad issues. One is what factors the formula should take into account. The other is whether there should be conditions attached.

With respect to the former issue, there are a number of possible factors that could be used, reflecting the need for public funding in the first place. In each case, the effect of the factor on institutional incentives is a concern. Three main factors are suggested by the principles. One is the cost of administrative overhead, which is a source of scale economies in PSE institutions. While in principle, it might be reasonable to include some element in the funding formula to account for this, actual administrative costs cannot be used because of the obvious incentive effects. Instead, there could be a fixed sum allocated to institutions based on something that is beyond the control of the institution.

Another element of funding could be related to the number of students, perhaps weighted by type of program. Again, the problem of incentives arises. A purely per capita funding formula gives an incentive for institutions to increase their student numbers. One may not want to avoid that incentive altogether, especially if some competition for students is regarded as beneficial on efficiency grounds. In any case, the government faces a conundrum. To the extent that per capita costs are a relevant component of the funding formula, but at the same time the government wants to temper the incentive to attract students, the student numbers used for funding each institution would have to be set by the government.

A final element of funding relates to the costs of doing research. This is a most difficult element to account for, especially as regards the proportion of faculty time devoted to research. Research costs are likely to vary significantly from institution to institution and from field to field. Moreover, the quality of research output is likely to as well. Given that an objective of public policy might be to improve the quality of research, funding could in principle be used as an incentive device for accomplishing that. For example, research funding could be partially related to indicators of research quality such as those obtained from peer review purposes. No doubt this would be controversial from the point of view of many faculty, who would argue that quantification of research output quality is fraught with difficulty. Nonetheless, some procedure must be used to allocate funding for research, and it could be argued that peer-reviewed quality indicators should play some role.[2]

The above discussion talks about costs without making the distinction between capital costs and operating costs. The presumption is that capital costing should be incorporated into the funding formula using standard techniques that take account of financing, depreciation and maintenance costs associated with investment in institutional infrastructure. On the other hand, most of these techniques presume that users can borrow to finance capital acquisitions. Whether or not borrowing is allowed and what rules should be applied to it are themselves important policy issues that have a bearing on institutional autonomy and the possibilities of future bailout requirements. To the extent that borrowing is not freely allowed, it may be necessary to have a separate source of capital financing for institutions, which would complicate matters even further.

The second broad issue concerns the conditionality of PSE funding. In principle, the government could use funding to institutions as a means of exercising influence on their spending priorities. That is, full funding could be made conditional on the institutions abiding by certain conditions. The analogue here might be conditions that the federal government attaches to general transfers to the provinces for health care. Conditions could include restrictions on degree programs to be offered, enrolments, accessibility criteria, or mobility requirements whereby students could move from one institution to another under certain conditions. Designing the appropriate set of conditions would require some thought. An obvious concern would be that the more detailed the conditions, the less autonomy would the institutions have.

Role of Institutions in Serving Needy Students. Finally, if governments have as an objective ensuring that needy students have equal access to higher education, the institutions may have some role in achieving that objective. We say "may" because one could argue that all issues of accessibility should be addressed by the financing of students rather than institutions. If that were the case, PSE institutions could be required simply to decide on admissions without reference to the need or income of the students or their parents, something that could be made a condition of government financing.

---

[2]The scheme of institutional research evaluation used in the United Kingdom is a possible model for this.

There is a strong argument for addressing needs via government aid to students rather than relying on institutions to deal with need. The government is much better placed to assess need than are the institutions, given their access to income tax records and their ability to compel students to provide the needed information in order to be eligible for assistance. In addition, one can argue that institutions do not have the right incentives to ensure that needs are dealt with on an interest-free and objective basis. Indeed, one can argue that current provincial government policies that compel universities to devote a proportion of fee increases to student aid are misguided. They serve to turn the universities into welfare-type agencies, a role for which they are not particularly well suited. The Rae Report seems to have embraced this philosophy as well, albeit not in much detail.

Institutions might also provide student aid to more meritorious students via scholarships. In this case, the institutions are presumably in a better position to evaluate merit. And, competition for students using scholarships may well be beneficial for the system as a whole to the extent that it precludes stratified outcomes in which students allocate themselves to universities according to their merit. In any case, scholarships tend to be financed by university endowments, and it would be difficult and undesirable for government to undo the effects of those.

Role of Federal versus Provincial Governments

So far, we have talked about the government as a monolith without taking account of the fact that the provincial and federal governments are both involved in the financing of higher education. Part of the reason why the Rae Report may have been less than complete in dealing with these issues is that its mandate was aimed mainly at the role of the (Ontario) provincial government in PSE.

The Canadian federation is highly decentralized, and provincial governments have legislative responsibility for higher education. Nonetheless, the federal government has an interest in the way PSE is delivered, and it intervenes in various ways at the moment. Part of the Canada Social Transfer (CST) is intended to be a contribution to PSE spending, though it comes with no strings attached and is not allocated on any criteria that is related to PSE spending needs. The federal government is involved more directly in PSE, in terms of supporting both institutions and students. University research is supported by federal grants awarded competitively, and PSE institutions are eligible for infrastructure grants. As well, Canada Research Chairs (CRCs) are funded by the federal government. Student assistance is available through a federal student loan program, and Millennium Scholarships are awarded to highly qualified students. Federal scholarship funding is also available to graduate students on the basis of a competition adjudicated by academic experts. The federal government provides assistance to PSE students through tax credits for tuition and educational expenses, as well as through educational savings plans that allow parents to save for their children's education in a tax-sheltered way. These programs are also designed to favour lower-income families.

The rationale for federal government intervention into an area of provincial responsibility has not been carefully spelled out in the past, and has not been subject to the same kind of acrimony as in the case of health care. Indeed, it is not clear that it could withstand constitutional scrutiny if put to the test. The constitutional basis for federal policy rests on three arguments. One is section 36 of the Constitution Act, 1982, which in its first part commits the federal government and the provinces jointly to "promoting equal opportunities for the well-being of Canadians, furthering economic development to reduce disparity in opportunities, and providing essential public services of reasonable quality to all Canadians". A second is the federal spending power, which allows the federal government to make transfer payments to both individual Canadians and provincial governments in the national interest. The third is the unlimited power of the federal government to tax as it sees fit, which presumably includes designing the tax system in ways that influence PSE.

In exercising these powers, the federal government cannot usurp the provinces' power to legislate in areas of exclusive provincial jurisdiction. This tempers the use of the spending power, and precludes using it in a way that effectively amounts to federal program legislation. Thus, original federal attempts to legislate unemployment insurance, even though that is a transfer system, were ruled to be unconstitutional by the courts and led to a constitutional amendment. It is not at all obvious that federal PSE programs, such as CRCs and grants for research or study, could pass the constitutional test. This is especially so when one realizes that some of the federal programs also exist in parallel form at the provincial level.

There may also be economic arguments for federal intervention in PSE. On efficiency grounds, the interprovincial mobility of both PSE students and graduates implies that there are spillovers from one province to another that can potentially lead to inefficient provincial decision-making. We can see examples of this in differential fees for out-of-province students as well as preferential admissions standards. There may also be arguments for harmonizing certain aspects of PSE, such as degree requirements and program content for professional programs. Perhaps most important, mobility guarantees could be built into all student assistance programs, including scholarships, loans, and grants. The research activities of universities can be regarded as more national than provincial in nature. To the extent that these function using peer evaluation, there are obvious advantages to the relevant peer group being national rather than provincial.

Equity considerations might also suggest a federal interest. To the extent that equity is regarded as a national concern, the federal government may have an interest in some degree of commonality with respect to accessibility to PSE and the relative sizes of student distributions across provinces. Federal transfers through the CST and Equalization programs go some way to ensuring that provinces have the fiscal capacity to provide comparable PSE programs. However, different provincial needs are not built into either program. The CST is basically an equal per capita transfer independent of student populations or costs, while Equalization equalizes revenue-raising capacity among recipient provinces.

At the same time, strong arguments can be made for provinces having the autonomy to design their PSE programs to suit their own needs and preferences. Indeed, this principle is well-entrenched in Canadian federalism practice with its heavy reliance on decentralization of programs in the areas of education, health, and welfare. The compromise that has been used in health and to some extent welfare is to leave program design and implementation with the provinces with federal support coming largely in the form of bloc grants with fairly general conditions attached. More direct federal programs in the provision of health and welfare services have been largely avoided. Indeed, in the area of elementary and secondary education, federal fiscal intervention has been even more muted. The Equalization program, which has no conditions, is the main source of federal support for this. These contrast with the case of PSE where, as mentioned, the federal government is directly involved in program delivery in some areas.

The main policy issue is the extent to which the model used in health and welfare ought to be used in PSE. One could imagine a system in which the federal role in PSE was restricted to a system of bloc grants with general conditions attached along the lines of the Canada Health Act. These conditions could include the kind of mobility provisions that we mentioned above. This bloc grant approach would avoid some of the duplication and

Robin Boadway

overlap of the current system, with the potential problems of accountability and cost-inefficiency that those might entail. It is not obvious, for example, that student assistance programs ought to exist at both levels of government. One could also argue that CRCs might be better administered by the provinces, perhaps supported by federal bloc funding. On the other hand, some functions have a national dimension to them, especially those involving research. Research grants and graduate student fellowships are national in scope and benefit from nationwide, or even international, peer reviewing. It may be difficult to achieve this national dimension in provincial programs.

In any case, some rationalization of the federal and provincial roles is desirable. The use of standard fiscal federalism instruments like federal grants and harmonization agreements would be part of that rationalization, as would a clearer definition of the division of responsibilities. Any comprehensive study of PSE policy should include consideration of both the federal and provincial roles. Again, the Rae Report has been relatively silent on that.

Final Comments on the Rae Report

Little has been said in this review about the details of the Rae Report. The reason is that the public finance content of the report is limited. There is no searching analysis of the economics of higher education and of the respective roles of government and the private sector in pursuing societal objectives. Without that, it is difficult to prescribe detailed policies, which the report makes little attempt to do. This was perhaps inevitable given the amount of time and resources available, and the fact that the mandate was limited to advice for the provincial government. Of course, this paper also falls far short of the kind of analysis that would be required to resolve policy issues facing a sector that is in desperate need of rebuilding. All that can be hoped for is that we have provided some sort of roadmap of the kinds of issues that must be faced in serious policy debates about the financing of higher education.

It might nonetheless be worth hazarding some remarks about some of the broad directions of reform. The current system seems to have evolved in a piecemeal fashion with incremental policy initiatives being implemented over a long period of time by both the provincial and federal governments. It seems clear that there is a need to rationalize the system of

PSE financing in several ways. We need to sort out how big the sector should be, especially how many places there should be for students of various sorts. Along with that, the share of financing borne by students needs to be determined. The system of student aid needs to be rationalized with equity and efficiency roles identified with particular financial instruments. If there is a desire to assist needy students, a policy instrument ought to be designed to achieve that objective, without equity being incorporated into all policy instruments. For example, a system of student grants based on need should be sufficient for achieving equity objectives rather than incorporating needs considerations into student loan programs, the tax system, tuition schedules, and so on. One could argue that the student loan system — or its analogues, income-contingent loans and graduate taxes — are essentially meant to improve the efficiency of student financing rather than to subsidize needy students. Given that, they should be self-financing and based on actuarial principles.

Grants to PSE institutions need also to be rationalized. Putting them on a longer-term basis, as the Rae Report recommends, is of course desirable. But designing their structure in a rational way is a precondition. More careful thought and analysis needs to go into choosing financing methods, which could include various elements. There could be a fixed component representing overhead costs that are only partly covered by tuition fees. There may be an element based on student numbers, though formulated in such a way that recognizes the implications, good or bad, that results from competing for students. There could be a component that reflects the quality of research that each institution is producing. Perhaps most important, the system of grants should reflect the balance between the autonomy of the institutions on the one hand, and the desire for oversight on the part of the government. Thus, autonomy can be promoted by making PSE institutions responsible for marginal revenues raised by tuition or other means, and not penalizing them for so doing. Oversight might be achieved by attaching conditions to institutional grants that induces them to abide by whatever provincial or national objectives are deemed important. There is nothing easy about designing an appropriate grant system that takes due account of both institutional needs, quality and incentives, but devoting some time and effort to the task seems like a co-condition, if not a pre-condition, to simply increasing the size of the grants.

Finally, and perhaps most pressing, is the need to rationalize the role of the federal and provincial governments in financing higher education. There is currently much duplication and overlap of programs, despite the fact that the provinces apparently have legislative responsibility for

Robin Boadway

education. Both the federal government and the provinces have programs of student assistance, loans, and scholarships. Both also provide support to the PSE institutions. While the provinces are largely responsible for providing operational funding, the federal government with programs like CRCs now contributes to that as well. The Rae Report has relatively little to say about this state of affairs, an omission that amounts to condoning it. Indeed, one of their recommendations invites the federal government to become more involved in student financing by calling on them to introduce a "substantial" federal program to cover the living costs of low-income and high-need students. Why student assistance should be divvied up between the federal and provincial governments so that the former is responsible for cost of living and the latter for tuition is not at all clear.

Rationalizing the system requires asking what is the national interest in PSE, and how can that best be achieved in a federal context in which the provinces deliver the product. One approach might be for the federal government to rely much more on bloc conditional transfers to the provinces rather than direct programs for students and institutions. These conditions could recognize important national concerns of student mobility and national equity objectives, such as those reflected in the constitution. This is the model that has worked reasonably well in the health and welfare sectors. Just as in the health sector, where the federal government assumes responsibility for some national aspect, such as public health and research, so in the PSE sector, it may have a more direct involvement in research, where the output is of national benefit and where national peer review processes are important. As well, the federal government will naturally be involved in measures that are delivered through the income tax system, though even here the provinces could play a major role. But it is not at all clear why the federal government needs to be involved in such direct programs as student scholarships, infrastructure investment, and even student loans.

These are the kinds of issues that need to be studied and resolved if a rational system of financing postsecondary education in Canada is to be put in place.

Reference

Roemer, J. 1998. *Equality of Opportunity*. Cambridge, MA: Harvard University Press.

Accessibility in the Rae Report

Lorne Carmichael

Ontario: A Leader in Learning, otherwise known as the Rae Report, was published in February 2005. The report has received overwhelmingly positive reviews from university administrators across the province, and many of its recommendations have been implemented wholly or partially, in the most recent provincial budget. But it has also been criticized for its failure to recommend that tuition rates be reduced or eliminated entirely. In fact the report recommends that individual universities have the discretion to raise tuition independently, so long as any increase is tied to increases in financial aid for those who need it.

The argument that any increase in tuition will inevitably reduce accessibility is a popular one with students and with some faculty, including those who are involved in the Ontario Council of University Faculty Associations (OCUFA). These commentators emphasize the difficulty some students have in affording the cost of university, and argue that student loan programs, even those that offer income-contingent repayment, do not help.

Bob Rae, a former NDP premier of Ontario, is a left-wing thinker with impeccable credentials. More important, he can also do arithmetic. He is clear in his rebuttal:

> Lurking behind some of the arguments against this new approach is the core objection that graduates, who have benefited from attending college or university, should not be expected to bear a reasonable share of the

costs of higher education. This is not a view that should detain us very long. (p. 22)

Rae does understand, of course, that high tuition creates a barrier for low-income students.

The remedy for that is not to increase the tuition subsidy for everyone, however. Rather, it is to focus attention on those whose need is greatest. The best way to ensure good access is to ensure that the institutions have the capacity to absorb a growing number of students and the resources to do a good job, to guarantee low income students grants and not just loans, and to address the "expectations barriers" to access much earlier in life. (p. 24)

With regard to accessibility, Bob Rae and his colleagues have gotten almost everything exactly right. If the report were implemented today in its entirety, the few small deficiencies would remain unnoticed and irrelevant given the many real improvements that would be gained.

In particular, the report is refreshingly clear and direct in acknowledging that higher education, for all its real public benefits, gives its private benefits overwhelmingly to the rich. Children from higher-income families are more likely to attend, and attending makes one more likely to earn a higher income later in life. We all agree that postsecondary education should be accessible to all students who stand to benefit, including those from the poorest of backgrounds. But to achieve this by making postsecondary education free to everyone would inflate even further the huge transfer of wealth that postsecondary education provides to the middle and upper classes, most of whom go to university anyway. This would be a huge waste of money given that there are other equally effective ways to ensure the participation of students from poorer backgrounds.

In this short comment I will outline what the Rae Report has to say about accessibility, and comment on some aspects where I may have something of value to say. An essay such as this one will inevitably find quibbles with the work that has been accomplished. But it should be clear that overall, I think the report is terrific. We should implement as much as possible as quickly as possible.

Capacity

There are two interrelated aspects to accessibility. The first might better be called "capacity". How many people should go to university? Rae believes the answer is "More than currently". His opinion is based on a claim that 70% of the new jobs in Ontario over the next few years will require some kind of postsecondary training. Accordingly, many of his recommendations — more graduate training, more money for infrastructure, more public support generally, controlled increases in tuition — are designed to increase accessibility by increasing capacity. He does not address the issue of where this new capacity should be built, although he does support a degree of increased competition among universities. This is explicit when it comes to distance education, which he believes should be expanded, and less explicit when he talks of allowing universities to set their own tuition.

In fact, the question of the optimal size for the university system has received surprisingly little attention. Some commentators will note that the average private return to a university degree is substantial, and will claim that there are further external benefits to society. Surely this means more people should be going to university. However, the optimal size of the system depends on the returns to education for the marginal student, not the average student. In other words, by expanding the system we will be bringing in less and less qualified students. We already admit some students who struggle and fail to complete their degrees. Do these students nonetheless benefit from their experience? Would they have been better off to attend a community college or some other training program? Will the external effects of educating a marginal student be as large as we might think they are for the average student? If we decide to change the curriculum so that weaker students can cope, can we do so without reducing the educational benefits received by the better students?

Current research does not provide good answers to these questions, but it is unfortunate that Rae does not address them at all. We know that some students get much better grades than others. We know that some graduates go on to earn a great deal of money and others do not. So it is clear that the average return to a university degree is higher than the marginal return. What we do not know is whether the marginal return is sufficiently high to warrant an expansion of the system.

Equal Access

The second aspect of accessibility involves ensuring that all students who are academically qualified can attend regardless of their ability to pay. There are different ways to achieve this, and it is important to note that some may actually reduce capacity. The most extreme position is that universities should be entirely free, with tuition and living expenses for students covered by the state. However, Rae notes that in countries where postsecondary education is free to the user the overall capacity of the system is often relatively small (Rae Report, p. 24), since the cost to government of a large system is great. Currently in Ontario, a move to make university tuition entirely free without a reduction in capacity would require about $2 billion per year in new public funding. To cover living expenses for students as well would clearly cost much more. In the end we could end up like our medical system, which is free to the user but still not fully accessible to qualified (i.e., genuinely sick) patients, despite massive public investment.

At the moment about half the current student population pays their tuition and living costs out of their own pockets. Some of these students work part-time while at school. Accessibility for the rest is provided in two ways — by allowing students to pay when they have the money and by charging the rich more than the poor for the same service. The former is accomplished through savings plans and loans with various repayment options, and the latter through targeted bursaries and grants to needy students.

Rae has many suggestions for improvements in each of these areas. He suggests the government provide a tuition grant, to a maximum of $6,000, to all students whose family income falls below a certain threshold, with universities required to top up this grant as needed if they raise tuition above this level. He wants to see information about loan programs centrally available to all students, loan limits increased, expected parental contributions reduced, and more flexible repayment options. Interest rates on these loans should be lower than at present. He would like to see a new loan program for the parents of students who do not qualify under the standard program. He wants to reach out to students from families where no one has yet gone to university. He would have the province join the federal government in augmenting private saving for university through targeted "learning bonds" for poorer families.

All of these are good ideas, and if implemented effectively they might be expected to have a real impact on accessibility. Indeed, one could perhaps fault the commission for neglecting to make any choices — it is as if any suggestion they thought might work has been recommended. We can go through some of the ideas in more detail.

There is a whole set of strategies that involve reaching out to potential students from poorer backgrounds. There should be a single Web portal where students can get all the information they need about available loans and grants and where they can apply for assistance. The Web site should also have information on career opportunities associated with each specialty, a great idea. Rae also wants to reach out to "first-generation" children — those who would be the first in their family to attend university. This is also a good idea but the practical difficulties of identifying these children may be problematic. Finally, he praises the federal government for introducing its "learning bond" initiative, which will help poorer families save for their children's education, and argues that the Ontario government should join this program. The program provides up to $4,000 for a child's Registered Education Savings Plan (RESP) account even if the parents contribute nothing else. The advantage (over a $4,000 targeted grant for first year tuition, say) is that it may promote "buy-in" and planning by the family for the education of their children. It is a good idea, but one waits for information about participation levels.

The suggested reforms to the student grant and loan system are similarly wide-ranging. The report calls for a move to increase direct grants to the lowest-income students, an increase in loan limits for those who do not get grants, a relaxation in the eligibility requirements for loans, a reduction in the required parental contribution, and most interesting, an extension of the program so that parents can get loans to cover their expected contributions. Again, one could perhaps wish that the commission had made some choices, but it's hard to fault any of these ideas. One minor oversight is that the suggested parental income cut-offs do not seem to account for families that might have more than one student in university at the same time.

The most controversial aspect of the student loan system involves income-contingent repayment (ICR). Currently there is some contingency since graduates with low incomes are sometimes able to negotiate relief, and others (about 7%) default on their loan. The commission would like to see an immediate move to a more formal loan forgiveness plan, and in the longer term to a loan plan where payments are based on income and made through payroll deduction, as in other countries such as Australia. This will require a great deal of federal/provincial cooperation since graduates move within Canada, and if their payments are to move with them they will have to be made federally.

Critics of income-contingent plans generally bring up two issues. The first is that by making repayment easier for low-income students, governments will find it easier to increase tuition rates and make education more expensive for all students. This was the argument that energized the opposition to a formal ICR plan some ten years ago in Canada, and such a plan was never implemented. Of course tuition rates have nonetheless risen substantially since then anyway. It is also clear that the private benefits to postsecondary education are substantial, so if one believes that increases in tuition are justified then the fact that an ICR will mitigate the effects on accessibility make this is an argument in favour of ICR.

The second argument is that those with lower incomes take much longer to pay off their loans, and so end up paying more money for their education than others. This argument is frustrating to an economist, since the present value of the repayment obligation is the same regardless of the repayment horizon. The argument boils down to a complaint that rich people have more money. Nonetheless the argument is persuasive for many people and may make implementation of an ICR plan more difficult.

The solution may be to move toward an all-encompassing graduate tax. In the limit this would incorporate both the grant and the loan portions of the current scheme into a system where tuition would be free for everyone while they attended university, but later on graduates would pay a specific tax based on the tuition cost of their program and their subsequent income. Students could then enter any program for which they are qualified, and those who go on to earn low incomes would pay less for the same program than those who earn more. The current grant system tries to accomplish much the same thing, but overall cost is based on family income at the time the student attends university rather than the lifetime income of the student.

The report is very realistic in its discussion of these issues, and is in fact quite subtle in its recommendations. It suggests that the provincial loan plan cover tuition only, and that a federal plan be focused on covering living expenses. The main reason for this is to avoid constitutional issues in federal/provincial mandates, but a genuine federal plan to cover living expenses could easily be made income contingent, and could be the first step to a more inclusive scheme. As well, the term "graduate tax" is never mentioned. Instead we are told about the merits of a "graduate benefit", even though this benefit is paid by graduates to government. Governments will presumably find it easier to introduce new benefits than new taxes.

One final recommendation is that the province reintroduce the Ontario Student Opportunity Trust Fund (OSOTF) by which the province agrees to match private capital donations for student bursaries. This recommendation runs somewhat counter to others that advocate a more streamlined approach to student support, since the OSOTF plan generates a plethora of university administered named fellowships with widely varying criteria for inclusion.

On balance, however, this is another good idea since like other plans to increase student support it may in the end allow universities more freedom in the way they spend their money. In general, universities are quite limited in the way they can spend, since governments and private donors like to see their money used in particular ways. It is only tuition revenue that is formally unrestricted, although a university charging very high tuition would be wise to devote significant resources to teaching.

Fundraising is a serious and challenging business, but raising money for students is perhaps the easiest of all. Revival of the OSOTF plan will make it easier still. So this program, and other programs to increase student financial aid, if they accommodate increases in tuition, may give universities more discretionary income without increasing the net cost to students or government.

Conclusions

The Rae Report calls for greater government support of universities, greater private support through increased tuition, and more effective and targeted support for those students who find the financial cost overwhelming. For those who understand the substantial private and public benefits that the university system creates, there can be little disagreement with any of these recommendations.

For those who would like to see postsecondary education provided entirely by the state, however, there is little comfort in the report. Some of these are students who may think they deserve something for nothing. Others are faculty who may wish to believe they are simple providers of learning and not, as well, integral components of the élite making machinery behind the modern economy. The report makes it abundantly clear that access can be provided to all students even when most must pay for a portion of their education. In so doing, Bob Rae has done a great service to postsecondary education in Ontario.

Contributors

Charles M. Beach is Professor in the Department of Economics and Director of the John Deutsch Institute at Queen's University.

Robin W. Boadway is Sir Edward Peacock Professor of Economic Theory in the Department of Economics at Queen's University.

H. Lorne Carmichael is Professor in the Department of Economics at Queen's University.

Michael L. Skolnik is William G. Davis Chair in Community College Leadership at the Ontario Institute for Studies in Education (OISE) of the University of Toronto.

Ken Snowdon is a higher education consultant, Snowdon & Associates Inc.

Queen's Policy Studies
Recent Publications

The Queen's Policy Studies Series is dedicated to the exploration of major policy issues that confront governments in Canada and other western nations. McGill-Queen's University Press is the exclusive world representative and distributor of books in the series.

John Deutsch Institute for the Study of Economic Policy

Current Directions in Financial Regulation, Frank Milne and Edwin H. Neave (eds.), Policy Forum Series no. 40, 2005 Paper ISBN 1-55339-072-5 Cloth ISBN 1-55339-071-7

Higher Education in Canada, Charles M. Beach, Robin W. Boadway and R. Marvin McInnis (eds.), 2005 Paper ISBN 1-55339-070-9 Cloth ISBN 1-55339-069-5

Financial Services and Public Policy, Christopher Waddell (ed.), 2004 Paper ISBN 1-55339-068-7 Cloth ISBN 1-55339-067-9

The 2003 Federal Budget: Conflicting Tensions, Charles M. Beach and Thomas A. Wilson (eds.), Policy Forum Series no. 39, 2004 Paper ISBN 0-88911-958-9 Cloth ISBN 0-88911-956-2

Canadian Immigration Policy for the 21st Century, Charles M. Beach, Alan G. Green and Jeffrey G. Reitz (eds.), 2003 Paper ISBN 0-88911-954-6 Cloth ISBN 0-88911-952-X

Framing Financial Structure in an Information Environment, Thomas J. Courchene and Edwin H. Neave (eds.), Policy Forum Series no. 38, 2003 Paper ISBN 0-88911-950-3 Cloth ISBN 0-88911-948-1

School of Policy Studies

Global Networks and Local Linkages: The Paradox of Cluster Development in an Open Economy, David A. Wolfe and Matthew Lucas (eds.), 2005 Paper ISBN: 1-55339-047-4 Cloth ISBN 1-55339-048-2

Choice of Force: Special Operations for Canada, David Last and Bernd Horn (eds.), 2005 Paper ISBN 1-55339-044-X Cloth ISBN 1-55339-045-8

Force of Choice: Perspectives on Special Operations, Bernd Horn, J. Paul de B. Taillon and David Last (eds.), 2004 Paper ISBN 1-55339-042-3 Cloth ISBN 1-55339-043-1

New Missions, Old Problems, Douglas L. Bland, David Last, Franklin Pinch and Alan Okros (eds.), 2004 Paper ISBN 1-55339-034-2 Cloth ISBN 1-55339-035-0

The North American Democratic Peace: Absence of War and Security Institution-Building in Canada-US Relations, 1867-1958, Stéphane Roussel, 2004 Paper ISBN 0-88911-937-6 Cloth ISBN 0-88911-932-2

Implementing Primary Care Reform: Barriers and Facilitators, Ruth Wilson, S.E.D. Shortt and John Dorland (eds.), 2004 Paper ISBN 1-55339-040-7 Cloth ISBN 1-55339-041-5

Social and Cultural Change, David Last, Franklin Pinch, Douglas L. Bland and Alan Okros (eds.), 2004 Paper ISBN 1-55339-032-6 Cloth ISBN 1-55339-033-4

Clusters in a Cold Climate: Innovation Dynamics in a Diverse Economy, David A. Wolfe and Matthew Lucas (eds.), 2004 Paper ISBN 1-55339-038-5 Cloth ISBN 1-55339-039-3

Canada Without Armed Forces? Douglas L. Bland (ed.), 2004 Paper ISBN 1-55339-036-9 Cloth ISBN 1-55339-037-7

Campaigns for International Security: Canada's Defence Policy at the Turn of the Century, Douglas L. Bland and Sean M. Maloney, 2004 Paper ISBN 0-88911-962-7 Cloth ISBN 0-88911-964-3

Institute of Intergovernmental Relations

Canadian Fiscal Federalism: What Works, What Might Work Better, Harvey Lazar (ed.), 2005 Paper ISBN 1-55339-012-1 Cloth ISBN 1-55339-013-X

Canada: The State of the Federation 2003, vol. 17, *Reconfiguring Aboriginal-State Relations,* Michael Murphy (ed.), 2005 Paper ISBN 1-55339-010-5 Cloth ISBN 1-55339-011-3

Canada: The State of the Federation 2002, vol. 16, *Reconsidering the Institutions of Canadian Federalism,* J. Peter Meekison, Hamish Telford and Harvey Lazar (eds.), 2004 Paper ISBN 1-55339-009-1 Cloth ISBN 1-55339-008-3

Federalism and Labour Market Policy: Comparing Different Governance and Employment Strategies, Alain Noël (ed.), 2004 Paper ISBN 1-55339-006-7 Cloth ISBN 1-55339-007-5

The Impact of Global and Regional Integration on Federal Systems: A Comparative Analysis, Harvey Lazar, Hamish Telford and Ronald L.Watts (eds.), 2003 Paper ISBN 1-55339-002-4 Cloth ISBN 1-55339-003-2

Available from: McGill-Queen's University Press
c/o Georgetown Terminal Warehouses
34 Armstrong Avenue
Georgetown, Ontario L7G 4R9
Tel: (877) 864-8477
Fax: (877) 864-4272
E-mail: orders@gtwcanada.com